Contents

The National Minimum Wage Act 1998

THE
Employment Acts

RICHARD HEMMINGS

PERTH COLLEGE
Learning Resource Centre

PERTH COLLEGE
LIBRARY

ACCN No: 007 01676	SUPPLIER: Dawson
CLASSMARK: 344.01	COST: £25-00
LOCATION: LOAN	DATE RECEIVED: 06/00

London: The Stationery Office

© The Stationery Office 1999

All rights reserved. No part of this publication may be reproduced, stored in a retrieval system, or transmitted in any form or by any means, electronic, mechanical, photocopying, recording or otherwise without the permission of the publisher.

Applications for reproduction should be made in writing to The Stationery Office Limited, St Crispins, Duke Street, Norwich NR3 1PD.

The information contained in this publication is believed to be correct at the time of manufacture. Whilst care has been taken to ensure that the information is accurate, neither the publisher nor the authors can accept responsibility for any errors or ommissions or for changes to the details given. Every effort has been made to trace copyright holders and to obtain permission for the use of copyright material. The publishers will gladly receive any information enabling them to rectify any errors or omissions in subsequent editions.

Richard Hemmings has asserted his moral rights under the Copyright, Design and Patents Act 1988, to be identified as the author of this work.

Crown copyright material reproduced with permission of Her Majestys Stationery Office

THE PUBLIC INTEREST DISCLOSURE ACT 1998

Index

The Employment Rights (Dispute Resolution) Act 1998
The National Minimum Wage Act 1998
The Public Interest Disclosure Act 1998, Explained

The Employment Rights (Dispute Resolution) Act 1998, the National Minimum Wage Act 1998 and the Public Interest Disclosure Act 1998 explained, was written by Richard Hemmings

His law firm - The Law Offices of Richard Hemmings LLM - specialises in employment law. During his first ten years in the profession he practised as a criminal defence advocate in East Anglia. By 1985 the level of employment law work enabled him to specialise exclusively in that field. He was fascinated by an area of law which was growing and changing rapidly as a result of year-on-year legislation by the Government and the significant impact of European law and the Decisions of the European Courts of Justice. At the same time the personnel function in many organisations was gaining long overdue respect as a worthy professional discipline in its own right

Richard is also an Employment Tribunal Chairman sitting part-time in London and a Consultant with Solicitors Taylor Vinters of Cambridge

The Law Offices of Richard Hemmings LLM

Sandy Lane
Barham
Ipswich
IP6 OPB

Tel: 01473 833844
Fax: 01473 833230

Web Site: http://www.hemmings.co.uk

Disclaimer

This publication is intended to provide a brief commentary on the Employment Rights (Dispute Resolution) Act 1998, the Minimum Wage Act 1998 and the Public Interest Disclosure Act 1998 and should not be relied upon by any part without taking further legal advice

Introduction

The aim of this book is to explain how the provisions of the Employment Rights (Dispute Resolution) Act 1998, the National Minimum Wage Act 1998 and the Public Interest Disclosure Act 1998 will affect those who are covered by their provisions.

The reader will be given a full understanding of the practical implications of the three Acts by means of comprehensive annotations to their provisions drawn from published and unpublished sources, Ministerial commitments and explanations and personal analysis in order to place these important additions to the body of employment law in context.

Employment law can be loosely defined as the collection of rules, enforceable in the Employment Tribunal, County Court or High Court, which governs what happens in the workplace. Legal rules do not exist in a vacuum. They have a purpose - primarily to strike a fair balance between the interests of an individual working within an organisation and the interests of the organisation benefitting from that person's skills and effort. What amounts to a fair balancing of competing interests at any particular point of time is judged by the Government of the day - politicians acting as social engineers to identify what is wrong and to fix it, either by changing the existing law (e.g. reducing the qualifying period for protection against unfair dismissal from two years to one year) or by introducing new law (e.g. the statutory right to paid annual leave introduced by the Working Time Regulations 1998).

The law is a precision tool in the hands of those lawyers who are expert in their field - craftsmen in their chosen specialisms. However the primary audience for the law is not lawyers but those affected by it - individuals and organisations. The law therefore needs to be accessible to non-lawyers and those advising them, particularly HR professionals, Trade Unions, CAB's and Law Centres. Accordingly, the explanatory notes alongside each clause are written in plain English. Although this necessarily involves a loss of the precision of the statutory text, the user-friendly purpose of this volume in the Points of Law series would otherwise by lost. The expert lawyer will undoubtedly move swiftly and confidently from the explanatory note into the familiar detail of statutory text. There will however be those for whom the explanatory notes meet their primary needs and only occasional reference to the statutory text will be required. For many readers starting with the explanatory note and moving into the statutory text as necessary will provide the knowledge and understanding they seek.

The Structure of this Guide

The next section of this chapter ("An Overview of the Acts") summarises the major provisions of the three Acts. It is intended to provide an introduction to the key provisions which will act as a constructive starting point for those unfamiliar with the legislation and as a refresher to the main components of the three Acts for those who already have a working knowledge of the legislation.

There then follows a copy of each Act with explanatory annotations. Wherever reference is made to a commencement date, there will be a related Commencement Order.

An Overview of the Acts

The Employment Rights (Dispute Resolution) Act 1998

In 1994 the Conservative Government commenced a review of the workings of Industrial Tribunals leading to the publication of a consultative Green Paper "Resolving Employment Rights Disputes : Options for Reform" in December 1994. Almost three and a half years later on 8 April 1998 the Employment Rights (Dispute Resolution) Act 1998 received Royal Assent with staggered implementation of its provisions.

In many respects the Act is merely enabling, providing the statutory power to introduce changes, the detailed provisions of which have subsequently emerged in part, whilst overall implementation has yet to be achieved.

The principal provisions are:

- Industrial Tribunals are renamed "Employment Tribunals" with consequential adjustments in other statutory provisions e.g. the Industrial Tribunals Act 1996 is renamed the Employment Tribunals Act 1996

- The Secretary of State is empowered to amend Employment Tribunal Procedure Regulations to permit Tribunals to determine cases, in specified circumstances, either without a hearing, or without hearing anyone other than one or both of the parties/their representatives. These circumstances include:

  - On written evidence only provided both parties consent;
  - After hearing only from the Applicant where the Respondent has done nothing to defend the complaint;
  - Hearing only from the Applicant where it appears that the Tribunal either has no power to grant the remedy sought or the complainant is not entitled to the remedy being sought;
  - Where on undisputed facts the Tribunal is bound by a prior decision of a Superior Court to dismiss the complaint;
  - On a preliminary hearing.

- Extending "sit alone cases" (i.e. where a Chairman generally must sit without lay members) to include the following complaints regarding the following:

  - Redundancy payments;
  - Written statements;
  - Guarantee payments;
  - Medical suspension;
  - Unauthorised or excessive deduction of Trade Union subscriptions;

- Non-payment of all or part of a protective award (under redundancy consultation rules);
- Non-payment of compensation for breach of the TUPE information/consultation rules.

- The creation of the post of "Legal Officers" to undertake routine interlocutory duties, and relieve the burden on Duty Chairmen (e.g. considering requests for postponements and time extensions, witness orders and dealing with formalities of signing-off cases withdrawn e.g. under an ACAS COT3 or a compromise agreement);

- A voluntary arbitration scheme to be established by ACAS, with the Secretary of State's approval, as an alternative means of resolving an unfair dismissal dispute;

- Extending the range of qualified advisers allowed to advise on compromise agreements beyond qualified lawyers to include approved and insured Trade Union officials and Advice Centre workers;

- Extending the conciliation role of ACAS to cover complaints regarding redundancy payments;

- Requiring Employment Tribunals to take into account, when assessing the compensatory award for unfair dismissal, an employee's failure to pursue an internal appeal, or the employer's obstruction of an employee from using any internal appeals procedure.

The National Minimum Wage Act 1998

The National Minimum Wage Act 1998 received Royal Assent on 29 July 1998 when its Regulation and Order making powers came into effect. The substantive provisions came into force on 1 April 1999, with some parts of the victimisation provisions operative from 1 November 1998.

The purpose of the Act is to establish a national minimum wage ("NMW") for the entire United Kingdom and all economic sectors. Because Agricultural Wages Boards survived the abolition in 1993 of the Wages Councils, which had set minimum rates of pay in certain sectors the Act will co-exist with the existing statutory framework for the Agricultural sector.

In many respect the Act is framework and enabling legislation in respect of which the National Minimum Wage Regulations 1999 SI.1999/584 provide the detailed working. These regulations were drafted and adopted in the light of the recommendations made by the Low Pay Commission. The National Minimum Wage Act 1998 (Amendment) Regulations 1999 SI.1999/583 came into force on 6 March 1999 and extended the regulation-making powers under s.3 of the Act to include those aged 26 years or over who are in the first six months of a new job with a new employer; participating in a scheme under which shelter is provided in return for work; on a training, work-experience or temporary work scheme; taking part in a scheme to help them find or get work; or on a sandwich course. The National Minimum Wage (Offshore Employment) Order 1999 extends the provisions of the Act and regulations to British and foreign workers who work in United Kingdom territorial waters or in certain circumstances in the UK or foreign sector of the continental shelf, mainly work on oil or gas rigs.

The key points of the Act are:

- The NMW is introduced at the rate of £3.60 an hour gross (£3 an hour gross for 18 to 21 years olds and £3.20 an hour gross for accredited trainees aged 22 or over in the first six months of a new job with a new employer);

- The Regulations prescribe the manner of calculating a worker's hourly rate of pay (and for this purpose what payments do and do not count in calculating the rate of pay and what time counts as working time for different categories of workers).

- Employers are obliged to pay eligible workers at or above the NMW to provide an NMW statement and to maintain records; however the statements-requirement has not been implemented following a change of Government policy;

- The Act gives the right to a NMW to all "workers" over school leaving age working in the United Kingdom subject to certain age and occupation/status related exceptions such as members of the Armed Forces, apprentices, share fishermen and voluntary workers. The Act applies to civil servants, Parliamentary staff and to most merchant seamen and to workers not employed on a contract of employment (but not the genuinely self-employed). There are also effective anti avoidance. There are also effective anti-avoidance measures to ensure that atypical workers such as agency temps without contracts and home-workers are entitled to the NMW;

- The Act protects eligible workers against unfair dismissal or being subjected to a detriment in circumstances related to their entitlement to the NMW;

- A worker can also make a complaint to the Employment Tribunal of an unauthorised deduction from wages or alternatively bring a civil action for breach of contract in the County Court where the burden of proof will be on the employer i.e. there will be a presumption that the claimant has been paid less than the NMW and it will be for the employer to prove otherwise;

- Enforcement officers have power to inspect records and order payment of arrears in cases of underpayment or to impose civil penalties on employers in persistent breach of the Act;

- In addition to claims being pursued by workers and enforcement officers the Act creates six new criminal offences. The successful prosecution of an employer will make them liable for a maximum fine of £5,000 in respect of each offence.

The DTI has a statutory obligation to publicise the NMW which has resulted in an advertising campaign with a £5m budget. The DTI has also prepared worthwhile guidance literature, established a Helpline on 0845 6000 678 and an enquiries address at NMW Enquiries, Freepost, PHQ1, Newcastle Upon Tyne.

A three year budget has been established to enforce the NMW through the Inland Revenue which has established a Task Force of including more than 60 Inspectors. The Government has also announced proposals to allow the Inland Revenue to pass to the Task Force information indicating breaches of the NMW discovered during inspections of employers' records and the Employment Relations Act permits this.

The Public Interest Disclosure Act 1998

The Public Interest Disclosure Act 1998 received Royal Assent on 2 July 1998 and its main provisions came into force on 2 July 1999. The Act was introduced as a Private Members Bill into the Commons by the Conservative MP Mr Richard Shepherd and into the Lords by the Labour Peer Lord Borrie QC, ultimately entering the statute book as result of Government commitment. The context for the legislation is the catalogue of major disasters and scandals in recent times where in many cases subsequent public enquiries have established that the knowledge existed to have averted or minimised the risk but that the culture of the organisation (fear or complacency) proved an insuperable obstacle to problems being addressed and resolved.

The Act introduces specific rights for those who disclose information to a third party about an alleged wrong doing in defined circumstances and protection against consequences such as unfair dismissal or being subjected to unlawful detriment.

The Act does not provide a general right of protection in respect of any kind of whistle blowing. The objective of the legislation is to direct the disclosures through appropriate channels. The Act has been applauded as providing the most comprehensive statutory whistle blower protection in the World. However, a disclosure will not attract the special protections in the Act unless it relates to one of the specified categories of subject matter and the disclosure is made in one of the specified manners of procedure.

Six categories of subject matter are:

- That a criminal offence has been committed, is being committed, or is likely to be committed;

- That a person has failed, is failing, or is likely to fail to comply with any legal obligation to which he or she is subject;

- That a miscarriage of justice has occurred, is occurring or is likely to occur;

- That the health or safety of any individual has been, or is being, or is likely to be endangered;

- That the environment has been, is being, or is likely to be damaged, or

- That information tending to show any matter falling within any one of the preceding paragraphs has been, is being, or is likely to be deliberately concealed.

However, disclosure will not qualify for protection if the person making the disclosure commits an offence by making it.

In addition, for the employee to obtain the protection of the Act, the disclosure must have been made in one of the six different ways set out in the Act:

- Disclosure to an employer or other responsible person;

- Disclosure to a legal adviser;

- Disclosure to a Minister of the Crown;

- Disclosure to a prescribed person (in respect of which the Public Interest Disclosure (Prescribed Persons) Order 1999 which came into force on 2 July 1999 applies);

- Disclosure in other cases where the worker makes the disclosure in good faith; reasonably believing the information and any allegations are substantially true; the disclosure is not made for personal gain; any one of the conditions following is met; and in all the circumstances of the case it is reasonable for the worker to make the disclosure.

The Act requires that certain specified factors must be borne in mind in determining whether or not it was reasonable for the worker to make the disclosure. The Act also provides a category of protected disclosure where the subject matter is serious enough to merit bypassing one of the other procedures provided the employee can show that the disclosure was made in good faith, reasonably believing that the information disclosed and any allegations contained in it are substantially true, the disclosure is not made for personal gain, the matter disclosed is of an exceptionally serious nature and it was reasonable for the worker to make the disclosure in all the circumstances. Provisions regarding the issue of reasonableness are set out in the Act.

The provisions regarding unfair dismissal and protection against unlawful detriment are grafted on to the Act and protect employees once it has been established that the subject matter and the manner of disclosure fall within the provisions of the Act.

The Public Interest Disclosure (Commencement) Order 1999 provides for the Act, so far as not already in force, to come into force on 2 July 1999. The Public Interest Disclosure (Compensation) Regulations 1999 removes the monetary limit, which s.124(1) of the Employment Rights Act 1996 imposes on the compensatory awards. Regulation 3 also provides for the payment of a higher additional award under s.117(3) of the Employment Rights Act 1996.

Employment Rights (Dispute Resolution) Act 1998

1998 c. 8

An Act to rename industrial tribunals and amend the law relating to those tribunals; to amend the law relating to dismissal procedures agreements and other alternative methods of resolving disputes about employment rights; to provide for the adjustment of awards of compensation for unfair dismissal in cases where no use is made of internal procedures for appealing against dismissal; to make provision about cases involving both unfair dismissal and disability discrimination; and for connected purposes.

[8th April 1998]

Be it enacted by the Queen's most Excellent Majesty, by and with the advice and consent of the Lords Spiritual and Temporal, and Commons, in this present Parliament assembled, and by the authority of the same, as follows:-

PART I

EMPLOYMENT TRIBUNALS

Renaming of tribunals

1.– (1) Industrial tribunals are renamed employment tribunals.

> **S.1(1)** - *The name of "Industrial Tribunals" is changed to "Employment Tribunals" with effect from 1 August 1998*

(2) Accordingly, the Industrial Tribunals Act 1996 may be cited as the Employment Tribunals Act 1996; and (wherever they occur in any enactment)-

> **S.1(2)** - *The Industrial Tribunals Act 1996 becomes the Employment Tribunals Act 1996. Statutory references to Industrial Tribunals becomes references to Employment Tribunals with effect from 1 August 1998*

    (a) for the words "industrial tribunal" substitute "employment tribunal",
    (b) for the words "industrial tribunals" substitute "employment tribunals",

(c) for the words "the Industrial Tribunals Act 1996" substitute "the Employment Tribunals Act 1996",

(d) for the words "President of the Industrial Tribunals (England and Wales)" substitute "President of the Employment Tribunals (England and Wales)", and

(e) for the words "President of the Industrial Tribunals (Scotland)" substitute "President of the Employment Tribunals (Scotland)".

Hearings etc.

2. In section 7 of the Employment Tribunals Act 1996 (which authorises the making of employment tribunal procedure regulations), after subsection (3) insert-

> **S.2** - *From 1 August 1998 the Secretary of State is empowered to make Employment Tribunal Procedure Regulations allowing Tribunals to decide cases on written evidence alone, i.e. without a hearing, or with only a limited hearing, in the following circumstances:*
>
> - *The Tribunal may dispense with an oral hearing, and determine the matter in private, where the parties have given their written consent - whether or not they subsequently withdraw it*
>
> - *The Tribunal may decide the case without hearing from anyone but the Applicant where:*
>
>   - *The person against whom the proceedings are brought has done nothing to contest the case*
>
>   - *It appears from the application that the Applicant is not seeking any relief which the Tribunal has power to give*
>
>   - *It appears from the application that the Applicant is not entitled to the relief being sought*
>
> *The Regulations can also be amended to allow the Tribunal to decide a case after hearing only from the Applicant and the Respondent (i.e. without hearing from witnesses) where:*
>
> - *On undisputed facts the Tribunal is bound by case law to dismiss the case of the Applicant or the Respondent; or*
>
> - *The proceedings relate only to a preliminary issue*
>
> *As at the publication date the Secretary of State has not introduced the Regulations under this section*

"(3A) Employment tribunal procedure regulations may authorise the determination of proceedings without any hearing (and in private) where the parties have given their written consent (whether or not they have subsequently withdrawn it).

(3B) Employment tribunal procedure regulations may authorise the determination of proceedings without hearing anyone other than the person or persons by whom the proceedings are brought (or his or their representatives) where-

(a) the person (or, where more than one, each of the persons) against whom the proceedings are brought has done nothing to contest the case, or

(b) it appears from the application made by the person (or, where more than one, each of the persons) bringing the proceedings that he is not (or they are not) seeking any relief which an employment tribunal has power to give or that he is not (or they are not) entitled to any such relief.

(3C) Employment tribunal procedure regulations may authorise the determination of proceedings without hearing anyone other than the person or persons by whom, and the person or persons against whom, the proceedings are brought (or his or their representatives) where-

(a) an employment tribunal is on undisputed facts bound by the decision of a court in another case to dismiss the case of the person or persons by whom, or of the person or persons against whom, the proceedings are brought, or

(b) the proceedings relate only to a preliminary issue which may be heard and determined in accordance with regulations under section 9(4)."

3.– (1) In section 4 of the Employment Tribunals Act 1996 (which makes provision about the composition of an employment tribunal), subsection (3) (which specifies the tribunal proceedings which are to be heard by the chairman alone unless he decides otherwise) is amended in accordance with subsections (2) to (5).

S.3 - *The categories of case where a Tribunal must consist only of a Chairman sitting alone, unless the Chairman exercises the discretion to allow the case to be heard by a full Tribunal of three are extended. The additional categories are:*

- *Unauthorised or excessive deductions of Trade Union subscriptions*

- *An employer's failure to pay remuneration under a protective award*

- *The right to receive a written statement of employment particulars, a statement of changes in particulars, and an itemised pay statement*

- *Guarantee payments*

- *Remuneration when suspended on medical grounds*

- *Redundancy payment*

- *An "employer's payment" against the Secretary of State*

> • *The appointment of an authorised person to conduct certain proceedings under the Employment Rights Act 1996 where the employee has died and has no personal representatives*
>
> • *A failure to pay compensation for non-compliance with the obligation to inform or consult over a transfer of an undertaking*
>
> *This section resolves a pre-existing uncertainty by also confirming that a Chairman sitting alone on a preliminary issue may hear evidence from witnesses. S.3 has effect where the date of the Tribunal hearing is first fixed on or after 1 August 1998*

(2) In paragraph (a) (which specifies proceedings under the Trade Union and Labour Relations (Consolidation) Act 1992)-

    (a) after "proceedings" insert "on a complaint under section 68A or 192 of the Trade Union and Labour Relations (Consolidation) Act 1992 or", and

    (b) for "the Trade Union and Labour Relations (Consolidation) Act 1992" substitute "that Act".

(3) In paragraph (c) (which specifies proceedings under the Employment Rights Act 1996)-

    (a) after "proceedings" insert "on a reference under section 11, 163 or 170 of the Employment Rights Act 1996,",

    (b) after "section 23" insert ", 34",

    (c) for "the Employment Rights Act 1996 or" substitute "that Act, on a complaint under section 70(1) of that Act relating to section 64 of that Act,", and

    (d) after "that" insert "Act or for an appointment under section 206(4) of that".

(4) After that paragraph insert-

"(ca) proceedings on a complaint under regulation 11(5) of the Transfer of Undertakings (Protection of Employment) Regulations 1981,"

(5) Omit paragraph (f) (which specifies proceedings in which the person bringing the proceedings has given written notice withdrawing the case), apart from the word "and".

(6) After subsection (6) of that section (which makes provision for employment tribunal procedure regulations to provide that any act required or authorised by the regulations to be done by a tribunal may be done by the chairman alone) insert-

" (6A) Subsection (6) in particular enables employment tribunal procedure regulations to provide that-

    (a) the determination of proceedings in accordance with regulations under section 7(3A), (3B) or (3C)(a),

(b) the carrying-out of pre-hearing reviews in accordance with regulations under subsection (1) of section 9 (including the exercise of powers in connection with such reviews in accordance with regulations under paragraph (b) of that subsection), or

(c) the hearing and determination of a preliminary issue in accordance with regulations under section 9(4) (where it involves hearing witnesses other than the parties or their representatives as well as where, in accordance with regulations under section 7(3C)(b), it does not),

may be done by the person mentioned in subsection (1)(a) alone."

4. In subsection (1) of section 4 of the Employment Tribunals Act 1996 (which provides that, subject to the following provisions of that section, employment tribunal proceedings are to be heard by the chairman and either two other members or, with the consent of the parties, one other member), for paragraph (b) substitute-

S.4 – *This section permits a Tribunal Chairman to sit with only one lay member rather than two as is usual provided the parties who are present or represented at the hearing agree. This reverses the former rule which required the consent of both parties even though one party might be absent and unrepresented and would be helpful on those occasions when a hearing would normally proceed in the absence of an unrepresented party who has failed to attend, but a lay member is also absent e.g. due to illness or travel disruption. At the time of publication this section has not yet been brought into force*

"(b) two other members selected as the other members in accordance with regulations so made or, with appropriate consent, one other member selected as the other member in accordance with regulations so made;

and in paragraph (b) "appropriate consent" means either consent given at the beginning of the hearing by such of the parties as are then present in person or represented, or consent given by each of the parties."

Other provisions

5. After subsection (6A) of section 4 of the Employment Tribunals Act 1996 (which is inserted by section 3(6) of this Act) insert-

> **S.5** - *The Secretary of State is empowered with effect from 1 August 1998 to provide that a legal officer, a new category of Tribunal official, may carry out various preliminary and interlocutory matters (i.e. the preparatory stages before the full merits hearing) in lieu of a Chairman i.e. any act that a Chairman may do sitting alone except a pre-hearing review. A legal officer may also determine proceedings if the parties agree. No regulations to implement this section have been made at the date of publication*

"(6B) Employment tribunal procedure regulations may (subject to subsection (6C)) also provide that any act which-

> (a) by virtue of subsection (6) may be done by the person mentioned in subsection (1)(a) alone, and
> (b) is of a description specified by the regulations for the purposes of this subsection,

may be done by a person appointed as a legal officer in accordance with regulations under section 1(1); and any act so done shall be treated as done by an employment tribunal.

(6C) But regulations under subsection (6B) may not specify-

> (a) the determination of any proceedings, other than proceedings in which the parties have agreed the terms of the determination or in which the person bringing the proceedings has given notice of the withdrawal of the case, or
> (b) the carrying-out of pre-hearing reviews in accordance with regulations under section 9(1)."

6. For section 87 of the Trade Union and Labour Relations (Consolidation) Act 1992 (which provides that a person who alleges that his employer has failed to comply with section 86 of that Act by wrongly deducting a political fund contribution or refusing to deduct union dues may make an application to a county court or sheriff court) substitute-

> **S.6** - *Complaints about a breach of s.86 Trade Union & Labour Relations (Consolidation) Act 1992 governing the deduction directly from wages of the proportion of Union dues which are payable (in respect of a Union's political fund) can be brought to an Employment Tribunal and not, as in the past, to the County Court or the Sheriff Court in Scotland. The transfer of jurisdiction applies where the date of payment of the relevant emoluments is on or after 1 August 1998*

" 87.– (1) A person who claims his employer has failed to comply with section 86 in deducting or refusing to deduct any amount from emoluments payable to him may present a complaint to an employment tribunal.

(2) A tribunal shall not consider a complaint under subsection (1) unless it is presented-

    (a) within the period of three months beginning with the date of the payment of the emoluments or (if the complaint relates to more than one payment) the last of the payments, or

    (b) where the tribunal is satisfied that it was not reasonably practicable for the complaint to be presented within that period, within such further period as the tribunal considers reasonable.

(3) Where on a complaint under subsection (1) arising out of subsection (3) (refusal to deduct union dues) of section 86 the question arises whether the employer's refusal to deduct an amount was attributable to the giving of the certificate or was otherwise connected with the duty imposed by subsection (1) of that section, it is for the employer to satisfy the tribunal that it was not.

(4) Where a tribunal finds that a complaint under subsection (1) is well-founded-

    (a) it shall make a declaration to that effect and, where the complaint arises out of subsection (1) of section 86, order the employer to pay to the complainant the amount deducted in contravention of that subsection less any part of that amount already paid to him by the employer, and

    (b) it may, if it considers it appropriate to do so in order to prevent a repetition of the failure, make an order requiring the employer to take, within a specified time, the steps specified in the order in relation to emoluments payable by him to the complainant.

(5) A person who claims his employer has failed to comply with an order made under subsection (4)(b) on a complaint presented by him may present a further complaint to an employment tribunal; but only one complaint may be presented under this subsection in relation to any order.

(6) A tribunal shall not consider a complaint under subsection (5) unless it is presented-

    (a) after the end of the period of four weeks beginning with the date of the order, but

    (b) before the end of the period of six months beginning with that date.

(7) Where on a complaint under subsection (5) a tribunal finds that an employer has, without reasonable excuse, failed to comply with an order made under subsection (4)(b), it shall order the employer to pay to the complainant an amount equal to two weeks' pay.

(8) Chapter II of Part XIV of the Employment Rights Act 1996 (calculation of a week's pay) applies for the purposes of subsection (7) with the substitution for section 225 of the following-

For the purposes of this Chapter in its application to subsection (7) of section 87 of the Trade Union and Labour Relations (Consolidation) Act 1992, the calculation date is the date of the payment, or (if more than one) the last of the payments, to which the complaint related."

PART II

OTHER METHODS OF DISPUTE RESOLUTION

Arbitration

7. After section 212 of the Trade Union and Labour Relations (Consolidation) Act 1992 insert-

> **S.7** - *This section, which came into force on 1 August 1998 provides the framework for ACAS to establish a scheme which give the parties to an unfair dismissal dispute the option of submitting the case to binding voluntary arbitration rather than using the Employment Tribunal. The Secretary of State may extend the category of claims that can be the subject of arbitration. ACAS issued a consultative document incorporating a draft scheme in July 1998. The target date of April 1999 for implementation has been missed and a pilot scheme in London for the autumn of 1999 followed by national implementation by April 2000, is the current proposal at the date of publication*

"212A.– (1) ACAS may prepare a scheme providing for arbitration in the case of disputes involving proceedings, or claims which could be the subject of proceedings, before an employment tribunal arising out of a contravention or alleged contravention of-

  (a) Part X of the (1996 c. 18.)Employment Rights Act 1996 (unfair dismissal), or
  (b) any enactment specified in an order made by the Secretary of State.

(2) When ACAS has prepared such a scheme it shall submit a draft of the scheme to the Secretary of State who, if he approves it, shall make an order-

  (a) setting out the scheme, and
  (b) making provision for it to come into effect.

(3) ACAS may from time to time prepare a revised version of such a scheme and, when it has done so, shall submit a draft of the revised scheme to the Secretary of State who, if he approves it, shall make an order-

  (a) setting out the revised scheme, and
  (b) making provision for it to come into effect.

(4) ACAS may take any steps appropriate for promoting awareness of a scheme prepared under this section.

(5) Where the parties to any dispute within subsection (1) agree in writing to submit the dispute to arbitration in accordance with a scheme having effect by virtue of an order under this section, ACAS shall refer the dispute to the arbitration of a person appointed by ACAS for the purpose (not being an officer or employee of ACAS).

(6) Nothing in the Arbitration Act 1996 shall apply to an arbitration conducted in accordance with a scheme having effect by virtue of an order under this section except to the extent that the order provides for any provision of Part I of that Act so to apply; and the order may provide for any such provision so to apply subject to modifications.

(7) A scheme set out in an order under this section may, in relation to an arbitration conducted in accordance with the law of Scotland, make provision-

(a) that a reference on a preliminary point may be made, or
(b) conferring a right of appeal which shall lie,

to the relevant court on such grounds and in respect of such matters as may be specified in the scheme; and in this subsection "relevant court" means such court, being the Court of Session or the Employment Appeal Tribunal, as may be specified in the scheme, and a different court may be specified as regards different grounds or matters.

(8) Where a scheme set out in an order under this section includes provision for the making of re-employment orders in arbitrations conducted in accordance with the scheme, the order setting out the scheme may require employment tribunals to enforce such orders-

(a) in accordance with section 117 of the Employment Rights Act 1996 (enforcement by award of compensation), or
(b) in accordance with that section as modified by the order.

For this purpose "re-employment orders" means orders requiring that persons found to have been unfairly dismissed be reinstated, re-engaged or otherwise re-employed.

(9) An order under this section setting out a scheme may provide that, in the case of disputes within subsection (1)(a), such part of an award made in accordance with the scheme as is specified by the order shall be treated as a basic award of compensation for unfair dismissal for the purposes of section 184(1)(d) of the (1996 c. 18.)Employment Rights Act 1996 (which specifies such an award as a debt which the Secretary of State must satisfy if the employer has become insolvent).

(10) An order under this section shall be made by statutory instrument.

(11) No order shall be made under subsection (1)(b) unless a draft of the statutory

instrument containing it has been laid before Parliament and approved by a resolution of each House.

(12) A statutory instrument containing an order under this section (other than one of which a draft has been approved by resolution of each House of Parliament) shall be subject to annulment in pursuance of a resolution of either House of Parliament."

8.– (1) In section 77 of the Sex Discrimination Act 1975 (subsection (3) of which prohibits contracting out of the provisions of that Act or the Equal Pay Act 1970, but subject to exceptions specified in subsection (4)), after subsection (4C) insert-

S.8 - *If the agreement to submit a dispute to arbitration under the ACAS scheme is made under the terms of a valid compromise agreement or after conciliation by an ACAS Conciliation Officer there will be no right to bring a claim before an Employment Tribunal under the Employment Rights Act 1996, the Sex Discrimination Act 1975, the Race Relations Act 1976, the Disability Discrimination Act 1995 or the Trade Union & Labour Relations (Consolidation) Act 1992 – commencement date 1 August 1998*

"(4D) An agreement under which the parties agree to submit a dispute to arbitration-

(a) shall be regarded for the purposes of subsection (4)(a) and (aa) as being a contract settling a complaint if-
   (i) the dispute is covered by a scheme having effect by virtue of an order under section 212A of the Trade Union and Labour Relations (Consolidation) Act 1992, and
   (ii) the agreement is to submit it to arbitration in accordance with the scheme, but
(b) shall be regarded for those purposes as neither being nor including such a contract in any other case."

(2) In section 72 of the Race Relations Act 1976 (subsection (3) of which prohibits contracting out of the provisions of that Act, but subject to exceptions specified in subsection (4)), after subsection (4C) insert-

"(4D) An agreement under which the parties agree to submit a dispute to arbitration-

(a) shall be regarded for the purposes of subsection (4)(a) and (aa) as being a contract settling a complaint if-
   (i) the dispute is covered by a scheme having effect by virtue of an order under section 212A of the Trade Union and Labour Relations (Consolidation) Act 1992, and

(ii) the agreement is to submit it to arbitration in accordance with the scheme,
but

(b) shall be regarded for those purposes as neither being nor including such a contract in any other case."

(3) In section 288 of the Trade Union and Labour Relations (Consolidation) Act 1992 (subsection (1) of which prohibits contracting out of the provisions of that Act, but subject to exceptions specified in subsections (2) and (2A)), after subsection (5) insert-

"(6) An agreement under which the parties agree to submit a dispute to arbitration-

(a) shall be regarded for the purposes of subsections (2) and (2A) as being an agreement to refrain from instituting or continuing proceedings if-
   (i) the dispute is covered by a scheme having effect by virtue of an order under section 212A, and
   (ii) the agreement is to submit it to arbitration in accordance with the scheme, but

(b) shall be regarded for those purposes as neither being nor including such an agreement in any other case."

(4) In section 9 of the Disability Discrimination Act 1995 (subsection (1) of which prohibits contracting out of the provisions of Part II of that Act, but subject to exceptions specified in subsection (2)), after subsection (5) insert-

"(6) An agreement under which the parties agree to submit a dispute to arbitration-

(a) shall be regarded for the purposes of subsection (2) as being an agreement not to institute, or an agreement not to continue, proceedings if-
   (i) the dispute is covered by a scheme having effect by virtue of an order under section 212A of the Trade Union and Labour Relations (Consolidation) Act 1992, and
   (ii) the agreement is to submit it to arbitration in accordance with the scheme, but

(b) shall be regarded as neither being nor including such an agreement in any other case."

(5) In section 203 of the Employment Rights Act 1996 (subsection (1) of which prohibits contracting out of the provisions of that Act, but subject to exceptions specified in subsection (2)), after subsection (4) insert-

"(5) An agreement under which the parties agree to submit a dispute to arbitration-

(a) shall be regarded for the purposes of subsection (2)(e) and (f) as being an agreement to refrain from instituting or continuing proceedings if-
   (i) the dispute is covered by a scheme having effect by virtue of an order under

section 212A of the Trade Union and Labour Relations (Consolidation) Act 1992, and

(ii) the agreement is to submit it to arbitration in accordance with the scheme, but

(b) shall be regarded as neither being nor including such an agreement in any other case."

Compromise agreements

9.– (1) In each of the provisions specified in subsection (2) (which provide that, for a compromise agreement to be valid, independent legal advice must have been received from a qualified lawyer), for "independent legal advice from a qualified lawyer" substitute "advice from a relevant independent adviser".

S.9 - *The source of qualifying advice for the purpose of a compromise agreement is extended beyond barristers and solicitors to include advice of non-lawyers provided they meet the criteria of "a relevant independent adviser".*

See Schedule One – Qualified lawyers and competent and properly insured TU officials and Advice Centre workers are relevant independent advisers – commencement date 1 August 1998

(2) The provisions referred to in subsection (1) are-

(a) section 77(4A)(c) of the Sex Discrimination Act 1975,

(b) section 72(4A)(c) of the Race Relations Act 1976,

(c) section 288(2B)(c) of the Trade Union and Labour Relations (Consolidation) Act 1992,

(d) section 9(3)(a) of the Disability Discrimination Act 1995, and

(e) section 203(3)(c) of the Employment Rights Act 1996.

10.– (1) In each of the provisions specified in subsection (2) (which provide that, for a compromise agreement to be valid, there must have been in force a policy of insurance covering the risk of a claim against the person who provided the advice about the agreement), for "policy of insurance" substitute "contract of insurance, or an indemnity provided for members of a profession or professional body,".

> **S.10** – *The earlier legislation required that for a compromise agreement to be valid, there must have been in force a policy of insurance covering the risk of negligent advice. This section changes the requirement for a "policy of insurance" by substituting "a contract of insurance, or an indemnity provided for members of a profession or professional body", placing beyond doubt the question of whether membership of the Solicitors' Indemnity Fund satisfies the insurance requirements for a compromise agreement. Prior to the implementation of this section on 1 August 1998 solicitors either relied on leading Counsel's opinion obtained by the Law Society that the Solicitors' Indemnity Fund satisfied the insurance criteria or appropriately qualified their certification of the compromise agreement*

(2) The provisions referred to in subsection (1) are-

    (a) section 77(4A)(d) of the Sex Discrimination Act 1975,

    (b) section 72(4A)(d) of the Race Relations Act 1976,

    (c) section 288(2B)(d) of the Trade Union and Labour Relations (Consolidation) Act 1992,

    (d) section 9(3)(b) of the Disability Discrimination Act 1995, and

    (e) section 203(3)(d) of the Employment Rights Act 1996.

Other provisions

11.– (1) In section 18(1) of the Employment Tribunals Act 1996 (which specifies the proceedings in relation to which the provisions about conciliation apply), in paragraph (d) (proceedings under the Employment Rights Act 1996), for "or 92," substitute ", 92 or 135,".

> **S.11** - *ACAS Conciliation Officers now have a duty to conciliate in claims relating to statutory redundancy payments – commencement date 1 October 1998*

(2) In section 166(2) of the (1996 c. 18.)Employment Rights Act 1996 (which defines "employer's payment" for the purposes of the provisions requiring the Secretary of State to make a payment to an employee whose employer is liable to pay him an employer's payment), after paragraph (a) insert-

"(aa) a payment which his employer is liable to make to him under an agreement to refrain from instituting or continuing proceedings for a contravention or alleged contravention of section 135 which has effect by virtue of section 203(2)(e) or (f), or".

(3) In section 168(1) of that Act (which specifies the amount which the Secretary of State is required to pay in respect of an employer's payment), after paragraph (a) insert-

"(aa) where the employer's payment to which the employee's application under section 166 relates is a payment which his employer is liable to make to him under an agreement having effect by virtue of section 203(2)(e) or (f), is a sum equal to the amount of the employer's payment or of any redundancy payment which the employer would have been liable to pay to the employee but for the agreement, whichever is less, and".

12.– (1) In section 110 of the Employment Rights Act 1996 (which provides that the statutory right not to be unfairly dismissed does not apply to employees covered by a designated dismissal procedures agreement), for subsection (2) (which provides that the statutory right nevertheless applies in the case of dismissals specified in certain statutory provisions) substitute-

> **S.12** - *This section amends s.110 of the Employment Rights Act 1996. S.110 provides that the statutory right not to be unfairly dismissed does not apply to employees covered by a designated dismissal procedures agreement, provided the agreement for arbitration provides the parties with the right to arbitration on a question of law. In practice, very few such agreements exist – commencement date 1 August 1998*

"(2) But if the agreement includes provision that it does not apply to dismissals of particular descriptions, subsection (1) does not apply in relation to a dismissal of any such description."

(2) In subsection (3) of that section (which specifies the matters as to which the Secretary of State must be satisfied before designating a dismissal procedures agreement), for paragraph (e) (which requires a dismissal procedures agreement to provide for arbitration or independent adjudication where a decision cannot otherwise be reached) substitute-

"(e) the agreement includes provision either for arbitration in every case or for-

  (i) arbitration where (by reason of equality of votes or for any other reason) a decision under the agreement cannot otherwise be reached, and
  (ii) a right to submit to arbitration any question of law arising out of such a decision, and".

(3) After subsection (5) of that section insert-

"(6) Where an award is made under a designated dismissal procedures agreement-

  (a) in England and Wales it may be enforced, by leave of a county court, in the same manner as a judgment of the court to the same effect and, where leave is given, judgment may be entered in terms of the award, and

(b) in Scotland it may be recorded for execution in the Books of Council and Session and shall be enforceable accordingly."

(4) In section 184 of that Act (which specifies the debts which the Secretary of State must satisfy if an employer has become insolvent), in subsection (1)(d) (which specifies a basic award of compensation for unfair dismissal payable by the employer), after "dismissal" insert "or so much of an award under a designated dismissal procedures agreement as does not exceed any basic award of compensation for unfair dismissal to which the employee would be entitled but for the agreement".

(5) The amendments made by subsections (1) and (2) do not affect any dismissal procedures agreement designated by the Secretary of State before those subsections come into force.

PART III

AWARDS OF COMPENSATION

13. After section 127 of the Employment Rights Act 1996 insert-

---

S.13 – *When assessing the amount of a compensatory award for unfair dismissal, the Employment Tribunal must reduce it by such amount as it considers just and equitable (not exceeding two weeks actual pay) where:*

- *The employer provided a procedure for appealing against dismissal*

- *The applicant at the time of dismissal or within a reasonable period afterwards was given written notice and details of the appeals procedure*

- *The applicant did not appeal against the dismissal under the procedure*

Correspondingly, where the employer provided a dismissal appeals procedure but prevented the employee from using it, the Employment Tribunal must include a supplementary award of such amount as it considers just and equitable, but not exceeding two weeks actual pay – commencement date 1 January 1999

"Internal appeal procedures. 127A.– (1) Where in a case in which an award of compensation for unfair dismissal falls to be made under section 112(4) or 117(3)(a) the tribunal finds that-

(a) the employer provided a procedure for appealing against dismissal, and

(b) the complainant was, at the time of the dismissal or within a reasonable period afterwards, given written notice stating that the employer provided the procedure and including details of it, but

     (c) the complainant did not appeal against the dismissal under the procedure (otherwise than because the employer prevented him from doing so),

the tribunal shall reduce the compensatory award included in the award of compensation for unfair dismissal by such amount (if any) as it considers just and equitable.

  (2) Where in a case in which an award of compensation for unfair dismissal falls to be made under section 112(4) or 117(3)(a) the tribunal finds that-

     (a) the employer provided a procedure for appealing against dismissal, but
     (b) the employer prevented the complainant from appealing against the dismissal under the procedure,

the award of compensation for unfair dismissal shall include a supplementary award of such amount (if any) as the tribunal considers just and equitable.

  (3) In determining the amount of a reduction under subsection (1) or a supplementary award under subsection (2) the tribunal shall have regard to all the circumstances of the case, including in particular the chances that an appeal under the procedure provided by the employer would have been successful.

  (4) The amount of such a reduction or supplementary award shall not exceed the amount of two weeks' pay."

14.– (1) In section 117(6) of the Employment Rights Act 1996 (which provides for a higher additional award for an unfairly dismissed employee who is not reinstated or re-engaged as ordered in a case where the dismissal is sex or race discrimination), at the end insert "and

> **S.14** - *The effect of this section is to prevent a successful applicant receiving, and an unsuccessful respondent paying, compensation twice in respect of action by the respondent which amounts both to disability discrimination and an unfair dismissal – commencement date 1 August 1998*

     (c) a dismissal which is an act of discrimination within the meaning of the Disability Discrimination Act 1995 which is unlawful by virtue of that Act."

  (2) Section 126 of that Act (which prohibits recovery under more than one provision in the case of an act which is both unfair dismissal and sex or race discrimination) is amended as follows.

  (3) In subsection (1) (which describes the circumstances in which the section applies), for paragraph (b) substitute-

"(b) any one or more of the Sex Discrimination Act 1975, the Race Relations Act 1976 and the Disability Discrimination Act 1995."

(4) In subsection (2) (which prohibits recovery under more than one provision)-

(a) omit "two or three", and
(b) for "the other, or any of the others," substitute "any other of them".

PART IV

SUPPLEMENTARY AND GENERAL

15. Schedule 1 (minor and consequential amendments) and Schedule 2 (repeals) have effect.

> **S.15** - *Provides for the minor and consequential amendments and repeals incorporated within Schedule I and Schedule II*

16. – (1) Subject to subsection (3), the preceding provisions of this Act (including the Schedules) do not extend to Northern Ireland.

> **S.16** - *This defines and limits the extent of the Act to Northern Ireland. The Employment Rights (Dispute Resolution) (Northern Ireland) Order 1998 No. 1265 (N.I.8) was laid before Parliament on 1 June 1998 and contains broadly comparable provisions*

(2) Section 1 does not have effect to amend any reference to a tribunal or office established under the law of Northern Ireland.

(3) Section 1(2) and Schedule 1 extend to Northern Ireland so far as they amend-

(a) the House of Commons Disqualification Act 1975,
(b) the Judicial Pensions Act 1981,
(c) the Tribunals and Inquiries Act 1992, and
(d) the Judicial Pensions and Retirement Act 1993.

(4) An Order in Council under paragraph 1(1)(b) of Schedule 1 to the (1974 c. 28.)Northern Ireland Act 1974 (legislation for Northern Ireland in the interim period) which contains a statement that it is made only for purposes corresponding to any of the purposes of this Act (other than those of section 1)-

(a) shall not be subject to paragraph 1(4) and (5) of that Schedule (affirmative resolution of both Houses of Parliament), but
(b) shall be subject to annulment in pursuance of a resolution of either House of Parliament.

17.– (1) The provisions of this Act (apart from section 16, this section and section 18 and paragraph 17(2) of Schedule 1) shall not come into force until such day as the Secretary of State may by order made by statutory instrument appoint; and different days may be appointed for different purposes.

> **S.17** - *Provides for commencement transitional provisions and savings*

(2) An order under subsection (1) may contain such transitional provisions and savings as appear to the Secretary of State to be appropriate.

(3) The amendment made by paragraph 17(2) of Schedule 1 shall be deemed always to have had effect.

(4) If an appeal of the sort which lie to the Employment Appeal Tribunal by virtue of the provision made by paragraph 17(2) of Schedule 1 has been brought before the High Court or the Court of Session not later than the day on which this Act is passed, the appeal may nevertheless be brought before the Employment Appeal Tribunal within the period of 42 days beginning with that day or such longer period as that Tribunal may by order specify.

18. This Act may be cited as the Employment Rights (Dispute Resolution) Act 1998.

> **S.18** - *This section defines the title of the Act as "The Employment Rights (Dispute Resolution) Act 1998"*

SCHEDULES

SCHEDULE 1

MINOR AND CONSEQUENTIAL AMENDMENTS

The Courts Act 1971 (c.23)

1. In Part IA of Schedule 2 to the Courts Act 1971 (which specifies the office-holders who are eligible for appointment as a circuit judge), for the entry beginning "President of Industrial Tribunals" substitute-

> *1. An amendment to the Courts Act 1971 consequential on the change of name from Industrial Tribunals to Employment Tribunals*

"President of the Employment Tribunals (England and Wales) or member of a panel of chairmen established by regulations under section 1(1) of the Employment Tribunals Act 1996 for employment tribunals for England and Wales."

The Sex Discrimination Act 1975 (c.65)

2. For section 77(4B) and (4C) of the Sex Discrimination Act 1975 substitute-

> *2. Amendments to the Sex Discrimination Act 1975 defining "a relevant independent adviser" for the purposes of the Act. A relevant independent adviser includes:*
>
> - *Qualified lawyers (including solicitors and barristers in practice and other authorised litigators or advocates e.g. certain legal executives)*
>
> - *Officers, officials, employees or members of an independent Trade Union provided the Union has certified in writing that the individual is both competent to give the advice and has been authorised to give advice on behalf of the Union*
>
> - *Advice Centre workers (volunteers and employees) certified and authorised as for Trade Union representatives*
>
> - *Others persons of a description specified in an Order made by the Secretary of State (no such Order having been made at the publication date)*
>
> *A person will be disqualified from acting as a relevant independent adviser in the following circumstances:*

- *If he or she is employed by or is acting in the matter for the other party or a person who is connected with the other party*

- *In the case of Union representatives and Advice Centre workers if the Union or Advice Centre is the other party or a person who is connected with the other party*

- *In the case of an Advice Centre worker (but not a Union representative or lawyer), if a payment is made for the advice received*

- *In the case of a person specified in an Order made by the Secretary of State if any condition specified in the Order is not met*

Note that there must be in force in relation to the relevant independent adviser, a contract of insurance or an indemnity provided that the members of a profession or professional body covering negligent advice. The other conditions relating to compromise agreements (that they must relate to the particular complaint(s), must state that the conditions regulating compromise agreements are satisfied, and must name the adviser), all continue to apply in this case and for other compromise agreements (paras 3, 11 and 24 below).

The original provisions in the Bill were much looser and the high degree of protective regulation was added, following widespread criticism, during the Committee stage in the House of Lords

"(4B) A person is a relevant independent adviser for the purposes of subsection (4A)(c)-

    (a) if he is a qualified lawyer,

    (b) if he is an officer, official, employee or member of an independent trade union who has been certified in writing by the trade union as competent to give advice and as authorised to do so on behalf of the trade union,

    (c) if he works at an advice centre (whether as an employee or a volunteer) and has been certified in writing by the centre as competent to give advice and as authorised to do so on behalf of the centre, or

    (d) if he is a person of a description specified in an order made by the Secretary of State.

(4BA) But a person is not a relevant independent adviser for the purposes of subsection (4A)(c) in relation to the complainant-

    (a) if he is, is employed by or is acting in the matter for the other party or a person who is connected with the other party,

    (b) in the case of a person within subsection (4B)(b) or (c), if the trade union or advice centre is the other party or a person who is connected with the other party,

(c) in the case of a person within subsection (4B)(c), if the complainant makes a payment for the advice received from him, or

(d) in the case of a person of a description specified in an order under subsection (4B)(d), if any condition specified in the order in relation to the giving of advice by persons of that description is not satisfied.

(4BB) In subsection (4B)(a) "qualified lawyer" means-

(a) as respects England and Wales, a barrister (whether in practice as such or employed to give legal advice), a solicitor who holds a practising certificate, or a person other than a barrister or solicitor who is an authorised advocate or authorised litigator (within the meaning of the Courts and Legal Services Act 1990), and

(b) as respects Scotland, an advocate (whether in practice as such or employed to give legal advice), or a solicitor who holds a practising certificate.

(4BC) In subsection (4B)(b) "independent trade union" has the same meaning as in the Trade Union and Labour Relations (Consolidation) Act 1992.

(4C) For the purposes of subsection (4BA) any two persons are to be treated as connected-

(a) if one is a company of which the other (directly or indirectly) has control, or

(b) if both are companies of which a third person (directly or indirectly) has control."

The Race Relations Act 1976 (c.74)

3. For section 72(4B) and (4C) of the Race Relations Act 1976 substitute-

> *3. Amendments to the Race Relations Act 1976 defining "a relevant independent adviser" for the purposes of the Act – adopting the definitions in Schedule 1.(2) above*

"(4B) A person is a relevant independent adviser for the purposes of subsection (4A)(c)-

(a) if he is a qualified lawyer,

(b) if he is an officer, official, employee or member of an independent trade union who has been certified in writing by the trade union as competent to give advice and as authorised to do so on behalf of the trade union,

(c) if he works at an advice centre (whether as an employee or a volunteer) and has been certified in writing by the centre as competent to give advice and as authorised to do so on behalf of the centre, or

(d) if he is a person of a description specified in an order made by the Secretary of State.

(4BA) But a person is not a relevant independent adviser for the purposes of subsection (4A)(c) in relation to the complainant-

(a) if he is, is employed by or is acting in the matter for the other party or a person who is connected with the other party,

(b) in the case of a person within subsection (4B)(b) or (c), if the trade union or adviccentre is the other party or a person who is connected with the other party,

(c) in the case of a person within subsection (4B)(c), if the complainant makes a payment for the advice received from him, or

(d) in the case of a person of a description specified in an order under subsection (4B)(d), if any condition specified in the order in relation to the giving of advice by persons of that description is not satisfied.

(4BB) In subsection (4B)(a) "qualified lawyer" means-

(a) as respects England and Wales, a barrister (whether in practice as such or employed to give legal advice), a solicitor who holds a practising certificate, or a person other than a barrister or solicitor who is an authorised advocate or authorised litigator (within the meaning of the Courts and Legal Services Act 1990), and

(b) as respects Scotland, an advocate (whether in practice as such or employed to give legal advice), or a solicitor who holds a practising certificate.

(4BC) In subsection (4B)(b) "independent trade union" has the same meaning as in the Trade Union and Labour Relations (Consolidation) Act 1992.

(4C) For the purposes of subsection (4BA) any two persons are to be treated as connected-

(a) if one is a company of which the other (directly or indirectly) has control, or

(b) if both are companies of which a third person (directly or indirectly) has control."

The Judicial Pensions Act 1981 (c.20)

4. In column 1 of the Table in section 16 of the Judicial Pensions Act 1981 (which provides a list of judicial offices for the purposes of provisions about lump sums, widows' pensions etc.), for the entry beginning "President of Industrial Tribunals" substitute-

4.   An amendment to the Judicial Pensions Act 1981 consequential on the change of name from Industrial Tribunals to Employment Tribunals

"Any office pensionable under section 12 of this Act".

5. In section 17(4) of that Act (which makes special provision about lump sums for certain offices), for "the office of President of Industrial Tribunals, or any other" substitute "any".

> **5.** *An amendment to the Judicial Pensions Act 1981 consequential on the change of name from Industrial Tribunals to Employment Tribunals*

The Courts and Legal Services Act 1990 (c.41)

6. In Schedule 11 to the Courts and Legal Services Act 1990 (which specifies judges who are barred from legal practice), for the entry beginning "President of Industrial Tribunals" substitute-

> **6.** *An amendment to the Courts and Legal Services Act 1990 consequential on the change of name from Industrial Tribunals to Employment Tribunals*

"President of the Employment Tribunals (England and Wales) or member of a panel of chairmen established by regulations under section 1(1) of the Employment Tribunals Act 1996 for employment tribunals for England and Wales".

The Trade Union and Labour Relations (Consolidation) Act 1992 (c.52)

7. After section 212A of the Trade Union and Labour Relations (Consolidation) Act 1992 (which is inserted by section 7 of this Act) insert-

> **7.** *An amendment to the Trade Union & Labour Relations (Consolidation) Act 1992 consequential on the amendment to dismissal procedures agreement*

"212B. ACAS may, in accordance with any dismissal procedures agreement (within the meaning of the Employment Rights Act 1996), refer any matter to the arbitration of a person appointed by ACAS for the purpose (not being an officer or employee of ACAS)."

8. In section 273(2) of that Act (which specifies the provisions which do not apply to persons in Crown employment), for "section 87(3) (power of court" substitute "section 87(4)(b) (power of tribunal".

> **8.** *An amendment to the Trade Union & Labour Relations (Consolidation) Act 1992 consequential on the transfer of jurisdiction in respect of the transfer to Tribunals of the political fund jurisdiction*

9.– (1) Section 288 of that Act (which restricts contracting out of the provisions of the Act) is amended as follows.

> **9.** *Amendments to the Trade Union & Labour Relations (Consolidation) Act 1992 defining "a relevant independent adviser" for the purposes of the Act – adopting the definitions detailed in Schedule 1.(2) above*

(2) In subsection (2B)(b) (which provides that a compromise agreement must relate to the particular complaint), for "complaint" substitute "proceedings".

(3) For subsections (4) and (5) substitute-

"(4) A person is a relevant independent adviser for the purposes of subsection (2B)(c)-

    (a) if he is a qualified lawyer,

    (b) if he is an officer, official, employee or member of an independent trade union who has been certified in writing by the trade union as competent to give advice and as authorised to do so on behalf of the trade union,

    (c) if he works at an advice centre (whether as an employee or a volunteer) and has been certified in writing by the centre as competent to give advice and as authorised to do so on behalf of the centre, or

    (d) if he is a person of a description specified in an order made by the Secretary of State.

(4A) But a person is not a relevant independent adviser for the purposes of subsection (2B)(c) in relation to the complainant-

    (a) if he is, is employed by or is acting in the matter for the other party or a person who is connected with the other party,

    (b) in the case of a person within subsection (4)(b) or (c), if the trade union or advice centre is the other party or a person who is connected with the other party,

    (c) in the case of a person within subsection (4)(c), if the complainant makes a payment for the advice received from him, or

    (d) in the case of a person of a description specified in an order under subsection (4)(d), if any condition specified in the order in relation to the giving of advice by persons of that description is not satisfied.

(4B) In subsection (4)(a) "qualified lawyer" means-

  (a) as respects England and Wales, a barrister (whether in practice as such or employed to give legal advice), a solicitor who holds a practising certificate, or a person other than a barrister or solicitor who is an authorised advocate or authorised litigator (within the meaning of the Courts and Legal Services Act 1990), and

  (b) as respects Scotland, an advocate (whether in practice as such or employed to give legal advice), or a solicitor who holds a practising certificate.

(4C) An order under subsection (4)(d) shall be made by statutory instrument which shall be subject to annulment in pursuance of a resolution of either House of Parliament.

(5) For the purposes of subsection (4A) any two persons are to be treated as connected-

  (a) if one is a company of which the other (directly or indirectly) has control, or

  (b) if both are companies of which a third person (directly or indirectly) has control."

10. In section 301(1) of that Act (which provides that that Act extends to England and Wales and Scotland), after "Wales and" insert "(apart from section 212A(6)) to".

> *10. An amendment to s.301(1) of the Trade Union & Labour Relations (Consolidation) Act 1992 excluding the operation of s.212 A(6)*

The Disability Discrimination Act 1995 (c.50)

11. For section 9(4) and (5) of the Disability Discrimination Act 1995 substitute-

> *11. Amendments to the Disability Discrimination Act 1995 defining "a relevant independent adviser" for the purposes of the Act – adopting the definitions detailed in Schedule 1.(2) above*

"(4) A person is a relevant independent adviser for the purposes of subsection (3)(a)-

  (a) if he is a qualified lawyer,

  (b) if he is an officer, official, employee or member of an independent trade union who has been certified in writing by the trade union as competent to give advice and as authorised to do so on behalf of the trade union,

(c) if he works at an advice centre (whether as an employee or a volunteer) and has been certified in writing by the centre as competent to give advice and as authorised to do so on behalf of the centre, or

(d) if he is a person of a description specified in an order made by the Secretary of State.

(4A) But a person is not a relevant independent adviser for the purposes of subsection (3)(a) in relation to the complainant-

(a) if he is, is employed by or is acting in the matter for the other party or a person who is connected with the other party,

(b) in the case of a person within subsection (4)(b) or (c), if the trade union or advice centre is the other party or a person who is connected with the other party,

(c) in the case of a person within subsection (4)(c), if the complainant makes a payment for the advice received from him, or

(d) in the case of a person of a description specified in an order under subsection (4)(d), if any condition specified in the order in relation to the giving of advice by persons of that description is not satisfied.

(4B) In subsection (4)(a) "qualified lawyer" means-

(a) as respects England and Wales, a barrister (whether in practice as such or employed to give legal advice), a solicitor who holds a practising certificate, or a person other than a barrister or solicitor who is an authorised advocate or authorised litigator (within the meaning of the Courts and Legal Services Act 1990), and

(b) as respects Scotland, an advocate (whether in practice as such or employed to give legal advice), or a solicitor who holds a practising certificate.

(4C) In subsection (4)(b) "independent trade union" has the same meaning as in the Trade Union and Labour Relations (Consolidation) Act 1992.

(5) For the purposes of subsection (4A) any two persons are to be treated as connected-

(a) if one is a company of which the other (directly or indirectly) has control, or

(b) if both are companies of which a third person (directly or indirectly) has control."

The Employment Tribunals Act 1996 (c.17)

12.– (1) Section 4 of the Employment Tribunals Act 1996 (which makes provision about the composition of an employment tribunal) is amended as follows.

12. *Amendments to the Employment Tribunals Act 1996 consequential on the changes to the composition of an Employment Tribunal*

(2) In subsection (1) (which provides that, subject to the following provisions of that section, tribunal proceedings are to be heard by the chairman and other members), after "Subject to the following provisions of this section" insert "and to section 7(3A)".

(3) In subsection (3)(a) (which specifies the tribunal proceedings under the Trade Union and Labour Relations (Consolidation) Act 1992 which are to be heard by the chairman alone unless he decides otherwise), after "68A" (which is inserted by section 3 of this Act) insert ", 87".

(4) In subsection (6) (which makes provision for employment tribunal procedure regulations to provide that any act required or authorised by the regulations to be done by a tribunal may be done by the chairman alone), for the words from ", in such circumstances" to "tribunal may" substitute "any act which is required or authorised by the regulations to be done by an employment tribunal and is of a description specified by the regulations for the purposes of this subsection may".

13. In section 5(1) of that Act (which provides for the payment of remuneration to the Presidents of the Employment Tribunals and to full-time chairmen of employment tribunals), at the end insert "and

13. *Amendments to the Employment Tribunals Act 1996 to provide remuneration for the new Tribunal post of "legal officer"*

(d) any person who is a legal officer appointed in accordance with such regulations,".

14.– (1) Section 7 of that Act (which authorises the making of employment tribunal procedure regulations) is amended as follows.

14. *Amendments to the Employment Tribunals Act 1996 consequential on the changes to authorisation under s.7 for the making of Employment Tribunal Procedure Regulations*

(2) Omit subsection (3)(f)(i) (which authorises the making of regulations about the persons entitled to appear and be heard on behalf of parties in tribunal proceedings).

(3) In subsection (4) (which provides that it is an offence to fail to comply with certain requirements imposed by an employment tribunal by virtue of regulations), after paragraph (b) insert ", or

(c) any requirement imposed by virtue of employment tribunal procedure regulations to give written answers for the purpose of facilitating the determination of proceedings as mentioned in subsection (3A), (3B) or (3C),".

15. In section 9(4) of that Act (which enables employment tribunal procedure regulations to provide that issues relating to the entitlement to bring or contest proceedings may be heard and determined in advance), for the words "any issue" onwards substitute "separately any preliminary issue of a description prescribed by the regulations which is raised by any case."

15. Amendments to the Employment Tribunals Act 1996 consequential on the changes to the scope for determining separately any preliminary issue

16. In section 18(1)(b) of that Act (which specifies the provisions of the Trade Union and Labour Relations (Consolidation) Act 1992 in relation to which the provisions about conciliation apply), after "68" insert ", 86".

16. Amendments to the Employment Tribunals Act 1996 consequential on the conciliation provisions in the Trade Union & Labour Relations (Consolidation) Act 1992

17.– (1) Section 21 of that Act (jurisdiction of the Employment Appeal Tribunal) is amended as follows.

17. A provision extending and clarifying the jurisdiction of the Employment Appeals Tribunal under s.21 of the Employment Tribunals Act 1996 - in particular confirming that the EAT has jurisdiction to hear appeals from Employment Tribunals in breach of contract disputes. This provision came into effect immediately on Royal Assent on 8.4.98 and applies retrospectively

(2) In subsection (1) (which specifies the decisions from which an appeal lies to the Employment Appeal Tribunal), at the end insert "or

(g) this Act."

(3) After subsection (3) insert-

"(4) The Appeal Tribunal also has any jurisdiction in respect of matters other than appeals which is conferred on it by or under-

(a) the Trade Union and Labour Relations (Consolidation) Act 1992,
(b) this Act, or
(c) any other Act."

The Employment Rights Act 1996 (c.18)

18. In section 23 of the Employment Rights Act 1996 (which makes provision for complaints to an employment tribunal in respect of unlawful deductions from wages etc.), at the end insert-

> *18. Amendments to the Employment Rights Act 1996 consequential on the changes regarding political fund jurisdiction*

"(5) No complaint shall be presented under this section in respect of any deduction made in contravention of section 86 of the Trade Union and Labour Relations (Consolidation) Act 1992 (deduction of political fund contribution where certificate of exemption or objection has been given)."

19. In section 112(4) of that Act (which provides for the making of an award of compensation for unfair dismissal in accordance with sections 118 to 127 where no order for reinstatement or order for re-engagement is made), for "127" substitute "127A".

> *19. Amendments to the Employment Rights Act 1996 consequential on the provisions regarding internal appeal procedures*

20. In section 117(3)(a) of that Act (which provides for the making of an award of compensation for unfair dismissal in accordance with sections 118 to 127 where a complainant is not reinstated or re-engaged in accordance with an order for reinstatement or an order for re-engagement), for "127" substitute "127A".

20. *Amendments to the Employment Rights Act 1996 consequential on the provisions regarding internal appeal procedures*

21.– (1) Section 118 of that Act (which provides that an award of compensation for unfair dismissal shall consist of a basic award, a compensatory award and, in certain cases, a special award) is amended as follows.

21. *Amendments to the Employment Rights Act 1996 consequential on the provisions regarding internal appeal procedures*

(2) In subsection (1)(b) (which provides that an award of compensation for unfair dismissal shall include a compensatory award calculated in accordance with sections 123, 124, 126 and 127), for "and 127" substitute ", 127 and 127A(1), (3) and (4)".

(3) After subsection (3) insert-

"(4) Where section 127A(2) applies, the award shall also include a supplementary award."

22. In section 122 of that Act (which makes provision for the reduction of the amount of a basic award of compensation for unfair dismissal), after subsection (3) insert-

22. *Amendments to the Employment Rights Act 1996 consequential on the changes regarding dismissal procedures agreements*

"(3A) Where the complainant has been awarded any amount in respect of the dismissal under a designated dismissal procedures agreement, the tribunal shall reduce or further reduce the amount of the basic award to such extent as it considers just and equitable having regard to that award."

23. In section 123(1) of that Act (which makes provision for the calculation of a compensatory award in accordance with that section but subject to sections 124 and 126), for "and 126" substitute ", 126, 127 and 127A(1), (3) and (4)".

23. *Amendments to the Employment Rights Act 1996 consequential on the provisions regarding internal appeal procedures*

24.– (1) Section 203 of that Act (which restricts contracting out of the provisions of the Act) is amended as follows.

> **24.** *Amendments to the Employment Rights Act 1996 defining "a relevant independent adviser" for the purposes of the Act – adopting the definitions detailed in Schedule 1.(2) above*

(2) In subsection (3)(b) (which provides that a compromise agreement must relate to the particular complaint), for "complaint" substitute "proceedings".

(3) For subsection (4) substitute-

"(3A) A person is a relevant independent adviser for the purposes of subsection (3)(c)-

    (a) if he is a qualified lawyer,

    (b) if he is an officer, official, employee or member of an independent trade union who has been certified in writing by the trade union as competent to give advice and as authorised to do so on behalf of the trade union,

    (c) if he works at an advice centre (whether as an employee or a volunteer) and has been certified in writing by the centre as competent to give advice and as authorised to do so on behalf of the centre, or

    (d) if he is a person of a description specified in an order made by the Secretary of State.

(3B) But a person is not a relevant independent adviser for the purposes of subsection (3)(c) in relation to the employee or worker-

    (a) if he is, is employed by or is acting in the matter for the employer or an associated employer,

    (b) in the case of a person within subsection (3A)(b) or (c), if the trade union or advice centre is the employer or an associated employer,

    (c) in the case of a person within subsection (3A)(c), if the employee or worker makes a payment for the advice received from him, or

    (d) in the case of a person of a description specified in an order under subsection (3A)(d), if any condition specified in the order in relation to the giving of advice by persons of that description is not satisfied.

(4) In subsection (3A)(a) "qualified lawyer" means-

    (a) as respects England and Wales, a barrister (whether in practice as such or employed to give legal advice), a solicitor who holds a practising certificate, or a person other than a barrister or solicitor who is an authorised advocate or authorised litigator (within the meaning of the Courts and Legal Services Act 1990), and

    (b) as respects Scotland, an advocate (whether in practice as such or employed to give legal advice), or a solicitor who holds a practising certificate."

25.– (1) Section 219 of that Act (which enables the making of regulations for preserving continuity of employment etc. in the case of a person who is dismissed and then reinstated or re-engaged in consequence of action to which subsection (2) of the section applies) is amended as follows.

> **25.** *Amendments to the Employment Rights Act 1996 altering the authority for the Secretary of State to make regulations preserving continuity of employment in the event of reinstatement or re-engagement*

(2) In subsection (1)-

    (a) omit ", in consequence of action to which subsection (2) applies,",
    (b) for "or re-engaged" substitute ", re-engaged or otherwise re-employed", and
    (c) at the end insert "in any circumstances prescribed by the regulations."

(3) Omit subsections (2) to (4).

26. In section 226(3) of that Act (which specifies the calculation date for a calculation for the purposes of section 119 or 121 which involves the notion of a week's pay), for "or 121" substitute ", 121 or 127A".

> **26.** *Amendments to the Employment Rights Act 1996 consequential on the changes regarding internal appeal procedures*

SCHEDULE 2

Section 15.

Repeals

Chapter	Short title	Extent of repeal
1992 c. 52.	The Trade Union and Labour Relations (Consolidation) Act 1992.	Section 88.
1993 c. 19.	The Trade Union Reform and Employment Rights Act 1993.	In Schedule 6, paragraph 4(b) and the word "and" preceding it.

Chapter	Short title	Extent of repeal
1996 c. 17.	The Employment Tribunals Act 1996.	In section 1(2), the words "; and the tribunals" onwards
		Section 4(3)(f), apart from the word "and"
		In section 5(1)(b), the word "and"
		Section 7(3)(f)(i)
		In section 21(1)(e), the word "or".
1996 c. 18.	The Employment Rights Act 1996.	In section 117, in subsection (6)(a), the word "and" and, in subsection (8), the words "(in accordance with sections 118 to 127)"
		In section 126(2), the words "two or three"
		In section 166(2)(a), the word "or"
		In section 168(1)(a), the word "and"
		In section 203(2)(f), the words "before an industrial tribunal"
		In section 219, in subsection (1), the words ", in consequence of action to which subsection (2) applies," and subsections (2) to (4)
		In Schedule 1, paragraph 56(5)
		In Schedule 2, in Part II, paragraph 18.

Self-explanatory table of repeals

National Minimum Wage Act 1998 (c. 39)

1998 c. 39

An Act to make provision for and in connection with a national minimum wage; to provide for the amendment of certain enactments relating to the remuneration of persons employed in agriculture; and for connected purposes.

[31st July 1998]

Be it enacted by the Queen's most Excellent Majesty, by and with the advice and consent of the Lords Spiritual and Temporal, and Commons, in this present Parliament assembled, and by the authority of the same, as follows:-

Entitlement to the national minimum wage

1.– (1) A person who qualifies for the national minimum wage shall be remunerated by his employer in respect of his work in any pay reference period at a rate which is not less than the national minimum wage.

> ***S.1(1)*** *- A qualifying person must be paid by his employer at least the National Minimum Wage ("NMW") in respect of work in any pay reference period*

(2) A person qualifies for the national minimum wage if he is an individual who-

> ***S.1(2)*** *- A person qualifies for the NMW if that person meets three conditions:*
>
> • *The individual is a worker;*
>
> • *The individual is working or ordinarily works in the United Kingdom*
>
> • *The individual has ceased to be of compulsory school age*

    (a) is a worker;
    (b) is working, or ordinarily works, in the United Kingdom under his contract; and
    (c) has ceased to be of compulsory school age.

(3) The national minimum wage shall be such single hourly rate as the Secretary of State may from time to time prescribe.

S.1(3) - The NMW is the single hourly rate set by the Secretary of State by order - Note: s.51(2) prevents the Regulations from providing differently "for different cases or for different descriptions of person" the effect of the two sections is that the Secretary of State by Regulations can both set the rate of the NMW and vary it periodically; and regional sectoral or other variations are not permitted

(4) For the purposes of this Act a "pay reference period" is such period as the Secretary of State may prescribe for the purpose.

S.1(4) - A pay reference period is the period set by the Secretary of State

(5) Subsections (1) to (4) above are subject to the following provisions of this Act.

S.1(5) - The above general entitlements and arrangements are subject to the detailed provisions in the Act

Regulations relating to the national minimum wage

2.– (1) The Secretary of State may by regulations make provision for determining what is the hourly rate at which a person is to be regarded for the purposes of this Act as remunerated by his employer in respect of his work in any pay reference period.

S.2 - The Secretary of State may make Regulations governing the way in which a worker's hourly rate is calculated for the purpose of establishing whether or not the national minimum hourly rate is being paid. These provisions are now set out in the National Minimum Wage Regulations SI.1999/584 ("the Regulations"). The Regulations provide for the treatment of a range of factors relevant to determining the hourly rate e.g. variable working patterns, the value of benefits in kind, paid and unpaid periods of lay-off. For the purpose of the scope of this section the Secretary of State is prohibited from making Regulations which result in differential treatment in relation to geographical location, employment sectors, the size of undertakings, age or occupation

(2) The regulations may make provision for determining the hourly rate in cases where-

(a) the remuneration, to the extent that it is at a periodic rate, is at a single rate;
(b) the remuneration is, in whole or in part, at different rates applicable at different times or in different circumstances;
(c) the remuneration is, in whole or in part, otherwise than at a periodic rate or rates;
(d) the remuneration consists, in whole or in part, of benefits in kind.

(3) The regulations may make provision with respect to-

(a) circumstances in which, times at which, or the time for which, a person is to be treated as, or as not, working, and the extent to which a person is to be so treated;
(b) the treatment of periods of paid or unpaid absence from, or lack of, work and of remuneration in respect of such periods.

(4) The provision that may be made by virtue of paragraph (a) of subsection (3) above includes provision for or in connection with-

(a) treating a person as, or as not, working for a maximum or minimum time, or for a proportion of the time, in any period;
(b) determining any matter to which that paragraph relates by reference to the terms of an agreement.

(5) The regulations may make provision with respect to-

(a) what is to be treated as, or as not, forming part of a person's remuneration, and the extent to which it is to be so treated;
(b) the valuation of benefits in kind;
(c) the treatment of deductions from earnings;
(d) the treatment of any charges or expenses which a person is required to bear.

(6) The regulations may make provision with respect to-

(a) the attribution to a period, or the apportionment between two or more periods, of the whole or any part of any remuneration or work, whether or not the remuneration is received or the work is done within the period or periods in question;
(b) the aggregation of the whole or any part of the remuneration for different periods;
(c) the time at which remuneration is to be treated as received or accruing.

(7) Subsections (2) to (6) above are without prejudice to the generality of subsection (1) above.

(8) No provision shall be made under this section which treats the same circumstances differently in relation to-

(a) different areas;

(b) different sectors of employment;
(c) undertakings of different sizes;
(d) persons of different ages; or
(e) persons of different occupations.

3.– (1) This section applies to persons who have not attained the age of 26.

> **S.3** - *The Secretary of State may exclude persons under the age of 26 from the Act altogether or set a different single hourly rate than the hourly rate set for the NMW*

(2) The Secretary of State may by regulations make provision in relation to any of the persons to whom this section applies-

(a) preventing them being persons who qualify for the national minimum wage; or
(b) prescribing an hourly rate for the national minimum wage other than the single hourly rate for the time being prescribed under section 1(3) above.

(3) No provision shall be made under subsection (2) above which treats persons differently in relation to-

(a) different areas;
(b) different sectors of employment;
(c) undertakings of different sizes; or
(d) different occupations.

(4) If any description of persons who have attained the age of 26 is added by regulations under section 4 below to the descriptions of person to whom this section applies, no provision shall be made under subsection (2) above which treats persons of that description differently in relation to different ages over 26.

4.– (1) The Secretary of State may by regulations amend section 3 above by adding descriptions of persons who have attained the age of 26 to the descriptions of person to whom that section applies.

> **S.4** - *The Secretary of State may extend the scope of s.3 by adding categories of persons notwithstanding that they have attained the age of 26. The National Minimum Wage Act 1998 (Amendment) Regulations 1999 SI.1999/583 came into force on 6 March 1999 and extended the regulation-making powers under s.3 of the Act to include those aged 26 years or over who are in the first six months of a new job with a new employer; participating in a scheme under which shelter is provided in return for work; on a training, work-experience or temporary work scheme; taking part in a scheme to help them find or get work; or on a sandwich course*

(2) No amendment shall be made under subsection (1) above which treats persons differently in relation to-

    (a) different areas;
    (b) different sectors of employment;
    (c) undertakings of different sizes;
    (d) different ages over 26; or
    (e) different occupations.

The Low Pay Commission

5.– (1) Before making the first regulations under section 1(3) or (4) or 2 above, the Secretary of State shall refer the matters specified in subsection (2) below to the Low Pay Commission for their consideration.

> *S.5 - The Secretary of State must refer certain matters to the Low Pay Commission ("LPC") before making the first Regulations. These include what single hourly rate should be set as the NMW; what period or periods should be set as the "pay reference period"; the means of calculating the hourly rate at which a person is to be regarded as remunerated; whether any, and if so what, provisions should be made of the Secretary of State's power to exclude or modify the NMW rules regarding those under the age of 26 and to what extent such category should be extended to include additional categories. The LPC is required to make a report to the Prime Minister and the Secretary of State. If the Secretary of State decides not to adopt the LPC's recommendations regarding any of the matters listed in sub-section 4 e.g. a different single hourly rate, the Secretary of State is obliged to lay reports before each House of Parliament stating the reasons. The LPC's recommendations are largely incorporated in the Regulations*

(2) Those matters are-

    (a) what single hourly rate should be prescribed under section 1(3) above as the national minimum wage;
    (b) what period or periods should be prescribed under section 1(4) above;
    (c) what method or methods should be used for determining under section 2 above the hourly rate at which a person is to be regarded as remunerated for the purposes of this Act;
    (d) whether any, and if so what, provision should be made under section 3 above; and
    (e) whether any, and if so what, descriptions of person should be added to the descriptions of person to whom section 3 above applies and what provision should be made under that section in relation to persons of those descriptions.

(3) Where matters are referred to the Low Pay Commission under subsection (1) above, the Commission shall, after considering those matters, make a report to the Prime Minister and the Secretary of State which shall contain the Commission's recommendations about each of those matters.

(4) If, following the report of the Low Pay Commission under subsection (3) above, the Secretary of State decides-

    (a) not to make any regulations implementing the Commission's recommendations, or

    (b) to make regulations implementing only some of the Commission's recommendations, or

    (c) to prescribe under section 1(3) above a single hourly rate which is different from the rate recommended by the Commission, or

    (d) to make regulations which in some other respect differ from the recommendations of the Commission, or

    (e) to make regulations which do not relate to a recommendation of the Commission,

the Secretary of State shall lay a report before each House of Parliament containing a statement of the reasons for the decision.

(5) If the Low Pay Commission fail to make their report under subsection (3) above within the time allowed for doing so under section 7 below, any power of the Secretary of State to make regulations under this Act shall be exercisable as if subsection (1) above had not been enacted.

6.– (1) The Secretary of State may at any time refer to the Low Pay Commission such matters relating to this Act as the Secretary of State thinks fit.

> **S.6** - *The Secretary of State may refer matters to the LPC at any time for it to consider and make recommendations*

(2) Where matters are referred to the Low Pay Commission under subsection (1) above, the Commission shall, after considering those matters, make a report to the Prime Minister and the Secretary of State which shall contain the Commission's recommendations about each of those matters.

(3) If on a referral under this section-

    (a) the Secretary of State seeks the opinion of the Low Pay Commission on a matter falling within section 5(2) above,

    (b) the Commission's report under subsection (2) above contains recommendations in relation to that matter, and

    (c) implementation of any of those recommendations involves the exercise of any power to make regulations under sections 1 to 4 above, subsection (4) of section 5 above shall apply in relation to the report, so far as relating to the recommendations falling within paragraph (c) above, as it applies in relation to a report under subsection (3) of that section.

(4) If on a referral under this section-

    (a) the Secretary of State seeks the opinion of the Low Pay Commission on any matter falling within section 5(2) above, but

    (b) the Commission fail to make their report under subsection (2) above within the time allowed under section 7 below,

the Secretary of State may make regulations under sections 1 to 4 above as if the opinion of the Commission had not been sought in relation to that matter.

7.– (1) This section applies where matters are referred to the Low Pay Commission under section 5 or 6 above.

> *S.7 - In making referrals to the LPC the Secretary of State may regulate the timetable for their report. The LPC is required to consult with representative organisations of employers and workers and at their discretion any other appropriate body. The LPC is required to have regard to the effect of the National Minimum Wage Act 1998 on the economy of the United Kingdom as a whole and on competitiveness and to take into account any additional factors as specified by the Secretary of State. The section also sets requirements for the content of reports from the LPC, for its reports to be laid before Parliament and published and defines "recommendations" and "report"*

(2) The Secretary of State may by notice require the Low Pay Commission to make their report within such time as may be specified in the notice.

(3) The time allowed to the Low Pay Commission for making their report may from time to time be extended by further notice given to them by the Secretary of State.

(4) Before arriving at the recommendations to be included in their report, the Low Pay Commission shall consult-

    (a) such organisations representative of employers as they think fit;

    (b) such organisations representative of workers as they think fit; and

    (c) if they think fit, any other body or person.

(5) In considering what recommendations to include in their report, the Low Pay Commission-

    (a) shall have regard to the effect of this Act on the economy of the United Kingdom as a whole and on competitiveness; and

    (b) shall take into account any additional factors which the Secretary of State specifies in referring the matters to them.

(6) The report of the Low Pay Commission must-

    (a) identify the members of the Commission making the report;

    (b) explain the procedures adopted in respect of consultation, the taking of evidence and the receiving of representations;

    (c) set out the reasons for their recommendations; and

    (d) if the Secretary of State has specified any additional factor to be taken into account under subsection (5)(b) above, state that they have taken that factor into account in making their recommendations.

(7) The Secretary of State shall-

    (a) lay a copy of any report of the Low Pay Commission before each House of Parliament; and

    (b) arrange for the report to be published.

(8) In this section-

"recommendations" means the recommendations required to be contained in a report under section 5(3) or 6(2) above, as the case may be;

"report" means the report which the Low Pay Commission are required to make under section 5(3) or 6(2) above, as the case may be, on the matters referred to them as mentioned in subsection (1) above.

The Low Pay Commission.

8.– (1) Subject to the following provisions of this section, the body which is to be regarded for the purposes of this Act as being the Low Pay Commission is the non-statutory Low Pay Commission.

> **S.8** - *This identifies and regulates the LPC*

(2) In this Act "the non-statutory Low Pay Commission" means the unincorporated body of persons known as "the Low Pay Commission" which was established by the Secretary of State after 1st May 1997 and before the passing of this Act for the purpose of making recommendations relating to the establishment, application and operation of a national minimum wage.

(3) The referral by the Secretary of State to the non-statutory Low Pay Commission at any time before the coming into force of this Act of matters (however described) corresponding to those specified in subsection (2) of section 5 above shall be treated as the referral required by subsection (1) of that section unless the Secretary of State otherwise determines.

(4) The referral by the Secretary of State to the non-statutory Low Pay Commission at any time before or after the coming into force of this Act, but before the

appointment of the body mentioned in subsection (9) below, of matters other than those mentioned in subsection (3) above shall be treated as a referral under section 6(1) above unless the Secretary of State otherwise determines.

(5) The report of the non-statutory Low Pay Commission (whether made before or after the coming into force of this Act) to the Prime Minister and the Secretary of State containing the Commission's recommendations about-

(a) the matters which are to be treated by virtue of subsection (3) above as referred under section 5(1) above, or

(b) the matters which are to be treated by virtue of subsection (4) above as referred under section 6(1) above,

shall be treated as the report of the Low Pay Commission under section 5(3) or 6(2) above, as the case may be, on the referral in question unless the Secretary of State, whether before or after the making of the report, makes a determination under subsection (3) or (4) above in relation to the referral.

(6) If, in the case of the matters described in subsection (5)(a) above or any particular matters such as are described in subsection (5)(b) above, the Secretary of State has, before the coming into force of this Act,-

(a) requested the non-statutory Low Pay Commission to make their report within a specified time, or

(b) having made such a request, extended the time for making the report,

the request shall be treated as a requirement imposed under subsection (2) of section 7 above and any such extension shall be treated as an extension under subsection (3) of that section.

(7) Accordingly, if-

(a) the Secretary of State has not made a determination under subsection (3) above, and

(b) the non-statutory Low Pay Commission fail to make the report required by section 5(3) above within the time allowed under this Act,

section 5(5) above applies.

(8) The non-statutory Low Pay Commission shall not be regarded as the body which is the Low Pay Commission for the purposes of this Act in the case of any referral under section 5(1) or 6(1) above which is made after-

(a) the non-statutory Low Pay Commission have made their report under section 5(3) above; or

(b) the time allowed under this Act to the non-statutory Low Pay Commission for making that report has expired without the report having been made; or

(c) the Secretary of State has made the determination under subsection (3) above.

(9) The Secretary of State may at any time appoint a body, to be known as "the Low Pay Commission", to discharge the functions conferred or imposed on the Low Pay Commission under this Act.

(10) Schedule 1 to this Act shall have effect with respect to the constitution and proceedings of the body appointed under subsection (9) above.

(11) Where the Secretary of State exercises the power conferred by subsection (9) above, the body which is to be regarded for the purposes of this Act as being the Low Pay Commission as respects the referral of any matter to the Low Pay Commission by the Secretary of State after the exercise of the power is the body appointed under that subsection.

(12) If the Secretary of State makes the determination under subsection (3) above, the power conferred by subsection (9) above must be exercised and the referral required by section 5(1) above must be made to the body appointed under subsection (9) above.

(13) If the Secretary of State makes a determination under subsection (3) or (4) above-

    (a) notice of the determination shall be given to the non-statutory Low Pay Commission; and

    (b) a copy of the notice shall be laid before each House of Parliament.

(14) No determination shall be made under subsection (3) or (4) above more than twelve months after the passing of this Act.

Records

Duty of employers to keep records.

9. For the purposes of this Act, the Secretary of State may by regulations make provision requiring employers-

> **S.9** - *The Secretary of State may make Regulations requiring employers to keep and preserve appropriate pay records*

    (a) to keep, in such form and manner as may be prescribed, such records as may be prescribed; and

    (b) to preserve those records for such period as may be prescribed.

Worker's right of access to records.

10. – (1) A worker may, in accordance with the following provisions of this section,-

> **S.10** - *A worker has the right to require his or her employer to produce any records which are relevant to establishing whether or not he or she has been paid at least the NMW and to inspect and copy those records. The worker must have reasonable grounds for believing that he or she is being paid less than the NMW; the worker must give the employer a written "production notice" requesting the production of any relevant records relating to such period set out in the notice, and the employer can set where the inspection takes place provided the worker is given reasonable notice of the place and time at which the records will be produced. Unless otherwise agreed, the employer must produce the records for inspection either at the worker's place of work or any other place at which it is reasonable, in all the circumstances, for the worker to attend. The relevant records must be produced within fourteen days of receipt of the production notice unless during that period the worker and the employer agree an extension of time. The worker has a right to be accompanied by a person of the worker's choice, when examining the records. If the worker intends to be accompanied, this must be stated in the production notice*

    (a) require his employer to produce any relevant records; and

    (b) inspect and examine those records and copy any part of them.

(2) The rights conferred by subsection (1) above are exercisable only if the worker believes on reasonable grounds that he is or may be being, or has or may have been, remunerated for any pay reference period by his employer at a rate which is less than the national minimum wage.

(3) The rights conferred by subsection (1) above are exercisable only for the purpose of establishing whether or not the worker is being, or has been, remunerated for any pay reference period by his employer at a rate which is less than the national minimum wage.

(4) The rights conferred by subsection (1) above are exercisable-

    (a) by the worker alone; or

    (b) by the worker accompanied by such other person as the worker may think fit.

(5) The rights conferred by subsection (1) above are exercisable only if the worker gives notice (a "production notice") to his employer requesting the production of any relevant records relating to such period as may be described in the notice.

(6) If the worker intends to exercise the right conferred by subsection (4)(b) above, the production notice must contain a statement of that intention.

(7) Where a production notice is given, the employer shall give the worker reasonable notice of the place and time at which the relevant records will be produced.

(8) The place at which the relevant records are produced must be-

    (a) the worker's place of work; or

    (b) any other place at which it is reasonable, in all the circumstances, for the worker to attend to inspect the relevant records; or

    (c) such other place as may be agreed between the worker and the employer.

(9) The relevant records must be produced-

    (a) before the end of the period of fourteen days following the date of receipt of the production notice; or

    (b) at such later time as may be agreed during that period between the worker and the employer.

(10) In this section-

"records" means records which the worker's employer is required to keep and, at the time of receipt of the production notice, preserve in accordance with section 9 above;

"relevant records" means such parts of, or such extracts from, any records as are relevant to establishing whether or not the worker has, for any pay reference period to which the records relate, been remunerated by the employer at a rate which is at least equal to the national minimum wage.

11. – (1) A complaint may be presented to an employment tribunal by a worker on the ground that the employer-

> *S.11 - Where an employer is breach of the provisions of s.10 e.g. by failing to produce the relevant records, or at the specified place, or within time, the worker's remedy is to present a complaint to the Employment Tribunal. The complaint must be presented within three months after the deadline for the production of the records, or if that was not reasonably practicable, within such further period as the Tribunal considers reasonable. A complaint may be heard by a Chairman sitting alone. If the Tribunal determines that the complaint is well-founded, it must make a declaration to that effect and award the worker the hourly rate of the NMW*

    (a) failed to produce some or all of the relevant records in accordance with subsections (8) and (9) of section 10 above; or

    (b) failed to allow the worker to exercise some or all of the rights conferred by subsection (1)(b) or (4)(b) of that section.

(2) Where an employment tribunal finds a complaint under this section well-founded, the tribunal shall-

    (a) make a declaration to that effect; and

(b) make an award that the employer pay to the worker a sum equal to 80 times the hourly amount of the national minimum wage (as in force when the award is made).

(3) An employment tribunal shall not consider a complaint under this section unless it is presented to the tribunal before the expiry of the period of three months following-

(a) the end of the period of fourteen days mentioned in paragraph (a) of subsection (9) of section 10 above; or

(b) in a case where a later day was agreed under paragraph (b) of that subsection, that later day.

(4) Where the employment tribunal is satisfied that it was not reasonably practicable for a complaint under this section to be presented before the expiry of the period of three months mentioned in subsection (3) above, the tribunal may consider the complaint if it is presented within such further period as the tribunal considers reasonable.

(5) Expressions used in this section and in section 10 above have the same meaning in this section as they have in that section.

12. – (1) Regulations may make provision for the purpose of conferring on a worker the right to be given by his employer, at or before the time at which any payment of remuneration is made to the worker, a written statement.

S.12 - The Secretary of State may make Regulations requiring employers to provide workers with an NMW statement to assist workers in determining whether they are being remunerated at a rate at least equal to the hourly rate of the NMW. The statement may be included in the written itemised pay statement required to be given by an employer under s.8 of the Employment Rights Act 1996 or Article 40 of the Employment Rights (Northern Ireland) Order 1996. The Regulations may provide for complaints to be referred to Employment Tribunals in Great Britain and Industrial Tribunals in Northern Ireland. However in February 1999 the Secretary of State announced that it had been decided to drop these requirements following consultation on draft Regulations, and the NMW Regulations do not include any requirements under this section

(2) The regulations may make provision with respect to the contents of any such statement and may, in particular, require it to contain-

(a) prescribed information relating to this Act or any regulations under it; or

(b) prescribed information for the purpose of assisting the worker to determine whether he has been remunerated at a rate at least equal to the national minimum wage during the period to which the payment of remuneration relates.

(3) Any statement required to be given under this section to a worker by his employer may, if the worker is an employee, be included in the written itemised pay statement required to be given to him by his employer under section 8 of the Employment Rights Act 1996 or Article 40 of the Employment Rights (Northern Ireland) Order 1996, as the case may be.

(4) The regulations may make provision for the purpose of applying-

    (a) sections 11 and 12 of the (1996 c. 18.)Employment Rights Act 1996 (references to employment tribunals and determination of references), or

    (b) in relation to Northern Ireland, Articles 43 and 44 of the (S.I. 1996/1919 (N.I.16).)Employment Rights (Northern Ireland) Order 1996 (references to industrial tribunals and determination of references),

in relation to a worker and any such statement as is mentioned in subsection (1) above as they apply in relation to an employee and a statement required to be given to him by his employer under section 8 of that Act or Article 40 of that Order, as the case may be.

Officers

13. – (1) The Secretary of State-

> *S.13 - The Secretary of State may appoint officers to enforce certain provisions of the Act and additionally or alternatively arrange for inspectors from existing Government Departments or agencies to act as enforcement officers. Enforcement officers must produce identification if requested when on duty and must identify themselves as an enforcement officer under the Act when on duty and dealing with someone who apparently is unaware of the fact. The Inland Revenue have been appointed to enforce the NMW with a staff of 125 including 63 Inspectors covering the United Kingdom*

    (a) may appoint officers to act for the purposes of this Act; and

    (b) may, instead of or in addition to appointing any officers under this section, arrange with any Minister of the Crown or government department, or any body performing functions on behalf of the Crown, that officers of that Minister, department or body shall act for those purposes.

(2) When acting for the purposes of this Act, an officer shall, if so required, produce some duly authenticated document showing his authority so to act.

(3) If it appears to an officer that any person with whom he is dealing while acting for the purposes of this Act does not know that he is an officer so acting, the officer shall identify himself as such to that person.

14. – (1) An officer acting for the purposes of this Act shall have power for the performance of his duties-

> *S.14 - Enforcement officers are authorised to require statutory records in accordance with Regulations made under s.9 to be produced to them when and where specified in the notice; to examine and copy such records; on reasonable written notice to require the records to be explained, either alone or in the presence of a witness at a time and place specified in the notice; on reasonable written notice to require any additional information which might reasonably be needed to establish compliance with the Act or any enforcement notice under s.19, the information to be provided to the enforcement officer at such time and place as specified in the notice; and to enter employer's premises "at all reasonable times" in order to exercise those powers. Enforcement officers may not require any person to answer questions or supply information which might incriminate that person or their spouse*

   (a) to require the production by a relevant person of any records required to be kept and preserved in accordance with regulations under section 9 above and to inspect and examine those records and to copy any material part of them;

   (b) to require a relevant person to furnish to him (either alone or in the presence of any other person, as the officer thinks fit) an explanation of any such records;

   (c) to require a relevant person to furnish to him (either alone or in the presence of any other person, as the officer thinks fit) any additional information known to the relevant person which might reasonably be needed in order to establish whether this Act, or any enforcement notice under section 19 below, is being or has been complied with;

   (d) at all reasonable times to enter any relevant premises in order to exercise any power conferred on the officer by paragraphs (a) to (c) above.

(2) No person shall be required under paragraph (b) or (c) of subsection (1) above to answer any question or furnish any information which might incriminate the person or, if married, the person's spouse.

(3) The powers conferred by subsection (1) above include power, on reasonable written notice, to require a relevant person-

   (a) to produce any such records as are mentioned in paragraph (a) of that subsection to an officer at such time and place as may be specified in the notice; or

   (b) to attend before an officer at such time and place as may be specified in the notice to furnish any such explanation or additional information as is mentioned in paragraph (b) or (c) of that subsection.

(4) In this section "relevant person" means any person whom an officer acting for the purposes of this Act has reasonable cause to believe to be-

(a) the employer of a worker;

(b) a person who for the purposes of section 34 below is the agent or the principal;

(c) a person who supplies work to an individual who qualifies for the national minimum wage;

(d) a worker, servant or agent of a person falling within paragraph (a), (b) or (c) above; or

(e) a person who qualifies for the national minimum wage.

(5) In this section "relevant premises" means any premises which an officer acting for the purposes of this Act has reasonable cause to believe to be-

(a) premises at which an employer carries on business;

(b) premises which an employer uses in connection with his business (including any place used, in connection with that business, for giving out work to home workers, within the meaning of section 35 below); or

(c) premises of a person who for the purposes of section 34 below is the agent or the principal.

Information

15. – (1) This section applies to any information obtained by an officer acting for the purposes of this Act, whether by virtue of paragraph (a) or paragraph (b) of section 13(1) above.

S.15 - Information obtained by an enforcement officer in the course of their duties remains the property of the employer but is held by the Secretary of State. Such information may be exchanged with the authorisation of the Secretary of State between difference agencies responsible for enforcing the NMW solely for purposes relating to the Act. It may be supplied to others only for the purpose of instituting civil or criminal proceedings under the Act with the authorisation of the Secretary of State

(2) Information to which this section applies vests in the Secretary of State.

(3) Information to which this section applies may be used for any purpose relating to this Act by-

(a) the Secretary of State; or

(b) any relevant authority whose officer obtained the information.

(4) Information to which this section applies-

(a) may be supplied by, or with the authorisation of, the Secretary of State to any relevant authority for any purpose relating to this Act; and

(b) may be used by the recipient for any purpose relating to this Act.

(5) Information supplied under subsection (4) above-

(a) shall not be supplied by the recipient to any other person or body unless it is supplied for the purposes of any civil or criminal proceedings relating to this Act; and

(b) shall not be supplied in those circumstances without the authorisation of the Secretary of State.

(6) This section does not limit the circumstances in which information may be supplied or used apart from this section.

(7) Subsection (2) above does not affect the title or rights of-

(a) any person whose property the information was immediately before it was obtained as mentioned in subsection (1) above; or

(b) any person claiming title or rights through or under such a person otherwise than by virtue of any power conferred by or under this Act.

(8) In this section "relevant authority" means any Minister of the Crown who, or government department or other body which, is party to arrangements made with the Secretary of State which are in force under section 13(1)(b) above.

16. – (1) This section applies to information which has been obtained by an officer acting for the purposes of any of the agricultural wages legislation.

S.16 - The exchange of information between agricultural wages officers and enforcement officers under the Act is authorised. This will enable an agricultural wages inspector who uncovers evidence of non-payment of the NMW to a worker who is not entitled to an agricultural minimum wage rate to refer such evidence to an enforcement officer. Correspondingly an enforcement officer who obtains evidence of non-payment of an agricultural minimum wage rate can pass the information to the Agricultural Wages Inspectorate

(2) Information to which this section applies may, with the authorisation of the relevant authority, be supplied to the Secretary of State for use for any purpose relating to this Act.

(3) Information supplied under subsection (2) above may be supplied by the recipient to any Minister of the Crown, government department or other body if-

(a) arrangements made between the recipient and that Minister, department or body under section 13(1)(b) above are in force; and

(b) the information is supplied for any purpose relating to this Act.

(4) Except as provided by subsection (3) above, information supplied under subsection (2) or (3) above-

(a) shall not be supplied by the recipient to any other person or body unless it is supplied for the purposes of any civil or criminal proceedings relating to this Act; and

(b) shall not be supplied in those circumstances without the authorisation of the relevant authority.

(5) This section does not limit the circumstances in which information may be supplied or used apart from this section.

(6) In this section-

"the agricultural wages legislation" means-

(a) the Agricultural Wages Act 1948;

(b) the Agricultural Wages (Scotland) Act 1949; and

(c) the Agricultural Wages (Regulation) (Northern Ireland) Order 1977;

"relevant authority" means-

(a) in relation to information obtained by an officer acting in England, the Minister of Agriculture, Fisheries and Food;

(b) in relation to information obtained by an officer acting in Wales, the Minister of the Crown with the function of appointing officers under section 12 of the Agricultural Wages Act 1948 in relation to Wales;

(c) in relation to information obtained by an officer acting in an area which is partly in England and partly in Wales, the Ministers mentioned in paragraphs (a) and (b) above acting jointly;

(d) in relation to information obtained by an officer acting in Scotland, the Minister of the Crown with the function of appointing officers under section 12 of the Agricultural Wages (Scotland) Act 1949; and

(e) in relation to information obtained by an officer acting in Northern Ireland, the Department of Agriculture for Northern Ireland.

Enforcement

17. – (1) If a worker who qualifies for the national minimum wage is remunerated for any pay reference period by his employer at a rate which is less than the national minimum wage, the worker shall be taken to be entitled under his contract to be paid, as additional remuneration in respect of that period, the amount described in subsection (2) below.

> ***S.17*** *- A worker who qualifies for the NMW and who is paid less than the NMW has a contractual right to recover the difference between what they have been paid and the NMW. Accordingly the worker may present a complaint to an Employment Tribunal under Part II of the Employment Rights Act 1996 (protection of wages unauthorised deductions) or if the employment has ended, for breach of contract. Alternatively an action in contract may be instituted in the County Court (or in Scotland, the Sheriff Court) where interest on damages is also recoverable*

(2) That amount is the difference between-

    (a) the relevant remuneration received by the worker for the pay reference period; and

    (b) the relevant remuneration which the worker would have received for that period had he been remunerated by the employer at a rate equal to the national minimum wage.

(3) In subsection (2) above, "relevant remuneration" means remuneration which falls to be brought into account for the purposes of regulations under section 2 above.

18. – (1) If the persons who are the worker and the employer for the purposes of section 17 above would not (apart from this section) fall to be regarded as the worker and the employer for the purposes of-

> ***S.18*** *- The scope of Part II of the Employment Rights Act 1996 (Protection of Wages) and Part IV of the Employment Rights (Northern Ireland) Order 1996 is extended to workers and employers who would not otherwise fall within Part II or Part IV for the purposes of s.17 of the Act*

    (a) Part II of the Employment Rights Act 1996 (protection of wages), or

    (b) in relation to Northern Ireland, Part IV of the Employment Rights (Northern Ireland) Order 1996,

they shall be so regarded for the purposes of the application of that Part in relation to the entitlement conferred by that section.

(2) In the application by virtue of subsection (1) above of-

    (a) Part II of the Employment Rights Act 1996, or

    (b) Part IV of the Employment Rights (Northern Ireland) Order 1996,

in a case where there is or was, for the purposes of that Part, no worker's contract between the persons who are the worker and the employer for the purposes of section 17 above, it shall be assumed that there is or, as the case may be, was such a contract.

(3) For the purpose of enabling the amount described as additional remuneration in subsection (1) of section 17 above to be recovered in civil proceedings on a claim in contract in a case where in fact there is or was no worker's contract between the persons who are the worker and the employer for the purposes of that section, it shall be assumed for the purpose of any civil proceedings, so far as relating to that amount, that there is or, as the case may be, was such a contract.

19. – (1) If an officer acting for the purposes of this Act is of the opinion that a worker who qualifies for the national minimum wage has not been remunerated for any pay reference period by his employer at a rate at least equal to the national minimum wage, the officer may serve a notice (an "enforcement notice") on the employer requiring the employer to remunerate the worker for pay reference periods ending on or after the date of the notice at a rate equal to the national minimum wage.

S.19 - An enforcement officer who believes that an employer has been paying at an hourly rate below the NMW is empowered to serve an enforcement notice on the employer requiring it to start paying the NMW to the relevant workers and to pay any appropriate arrears. An employer has a right of appeal to an Employment Tribunal within four weeks of receiving an enforcement notice. The appeal may be heard by a Chairman sitting alone. For the appeal to succeed the employer must show that the enforcement officer had no reason to serve any enforcement notice; or that the enforcement officer had no reason to include some of the workers concerned in the notice; or that no wage arrears were owed to the workers or that the alleged amount of the arrears is wrong. The Employment Tribunal will rescind the enforcement notice if the appeal is successful and any penalty notice served on the employer will be of no effect. If the appeal is only partially successful the Tribunal will correct the enforcement notice and any penalty notice. If the appeal is unsuccessful it will be dismissed. The Tribunal at its discretion may award costs against the enforcement officer if the enforcement officer acted unreasonably in the defence of the enforcement notice

(2) An enforcement notice may also require the employer to pay to the worker within such time as may be specified in the notice the sum due to the worker under section 17 above in respect of the employer's previous failure to remunerate the worker at a rate at least equal to the national minimum wage.

(3) The same enforcement notice may relate to more than one worker (and, where it does so, may be so framed as to relate to workers specified in the notice or to workers of a description so specified).

(4) A person on whom an enforcement notice is served may appeal against the notice before the end of the period of four weeks following the date of service of the notice.

(5) An appeal under subsection (4) above lies to an employment tribunal.

(6) On an appeal under subsection (4) above, the employment tribunal shall dismiss the appeal unless it is established-

(a) that, in the case of the worker or workers to whom the enforcement notice relates, the facts are such that an officer who was aware of them would have had no reason to serve any enforcement notice on the appellant; or

(b) where the enforcement notice relates to two or more workers, that the facts are such that an officer who was aware of them would have had no reason to include some of the workers in any enforcement notice served on the appellant; or

(c) where the enforcement notice imposes a requirement under subsection (2) above in relation to a worker,-

(i) that no sum was due to the worker under section 17 above; or

(ii) that the amount specified in the notice as the sum due to the worker under that section is incorrect;

and in this subsection any reference to a worker includes a reference to a person whom the enforcement notice purports to treat as a worker.

(7) Where an appeal is allowed by virtue of paragraph (a) of subsection (6) above, the employment tribunal shall rescind the enforcement notice.

(8) If, in a case where subsection (7) above does not apply, an appeal is allowed by virtue of paragraph (b) or (c) of subsection (6) above-

(a) the employment tribunal shall rectify the enforcement notice; and

(b) the enforcement notice shall have effect as if it had originally been served as so rectified.

(9) The powers of an employment tribunal in allowing an appeal in a case where subsection (8) above applies shall include power to rectify, as the tribunal may consider appropriate in consequence of its decision on the appeal, any penalty notice which has been served under section 21 below in respect of the enforcement notice.

(10)Where a penalty notice is rectified under subsection (9) above, it shall have effect as if it had originally been served as so rectified.

20. – (1) If an enforcement notice is not complied with in whole or in part, an officer acting for the purposes of this Act may, on behalf of any worker to whom the notice relates,-

S.20 - If an enforcement notice is not complied with the enforcement officer may present a complaint to an Employment Tribunal that the employer has made an unauthorised deduction from wages or take other civil proceedings to recover sums due to the workers

(a) present a complaint under section 23(1)(a) of the Employment Rights Act 1996 (deductions from worker's wages in contravention of section 13 of that Act) to an employment tribunal in respect of any sums due to the worker by virtue of section 17 above; or

(b) in relation to Northern Ireland, present a complaint under Article 55(1)(a) of the Employment Rights (Northern Ireland) Order 1996 (deductions from worker's wages in contravention of Article 45 of that Order) to an industrial tribunal in respect of any sums due to the worker by virtue of section 17 above; or

(c) commence other civil proceedings for the recovery, on a claim in contract, of any sums due to the worker by virtue of section 17 above.

(2) The powers conferred by subsection (1) above for the recovery of sums due from an employer to a worker shall not be in derogation of any right which the worker may have to recover such sums by civil proceedings.

21. – (1) If an officer acting for the purposes of this Act is satisfied that a person on whom an enforcement notice has been served has failed, in whole or in part, to comply with the notice, the officer may serve on that person a notice (a "penalty notice") requiring the person to pay a financial penalty to the Secretary of State.

S.21 - The enforcement officer may serve a penalty notice on the employer requiring it to pay a fine, no earlier than four weeks from the date it receives the notice, where the enforcement officer is satisfied that an employer has failed to comply with an enforcement notice. The amount of the fine is twice the hourly rate of the NMW, current when the penalty notice is served for each underpaid worker and each day of non-compliance. The fine is payable to the Secretary of State who is empowered by Regulation to adjust the amount by changing the multiplier. Unpaid fines are treated as judgment debts and are therefore recoverable without the need to prove the debt before a Court. This procedure is additional to the claim on behalf of the workers concerned under s.20

(2) A penalty notice must state-

(a) the amount of the financial penalty;
(b) the time within which the financial penalty is to be paid (which must not be less than four weeks from the date of service of the notice);
(c) the period to which the financial penalty relates;
(d) the respects in which the officer is of the opinion that the enforcement notice has not been complied with; and
(e) the calculation of the amount of the financial penalty.

(3) The amount of the financial penalty shall be calculated at a rate equal to twice the hourly amount of the national minimum wage (as in force at the date of the

penalty notice) in respect of each worker to whom the failure to comply relates for each day during which the failure to comply has continued in respect of the worker.

(4) The Secretary of State may by regulations from time to time amend the multiplier for the time being specified in subsection (3) above in relation to the hourly amount of the national minimum wage.

(5) A financial penalty under this section-

(a) in England and Wales, shall be recoverable, if a county court so orders, by execution issued from the county court or otherwise as if it were payable under an order of that court;

(b) in Scotland, may be enforced in the same manner as an extract registered decree arbitral bearing a warrant for execution issued by the sheriff court of any sheriffdom in Scotland;

(c) in Northern Ireland, shall be recoverable, if the county court so orders, as if it were payable under an order of that court.

(6) Where a person has appealed under subsection (4) of section 19 above against an enforcement notice and the appeal has not been withdrawn or finally determined, then, notwithstanding the appeal,-

(a) the enforcement notice shall have effect; and

(b) an officer may serve a penalty notice in respect of the enforcement notice.

(7) If, in a case falling within subsection (6) above, an officer serves a penalty notice in respect of the enforcement notice, the penalty notice-

(a) shall not be enforceable until the appeal has been withdrawn or finally determined; and

(b) shall be of no effect if the enforcement notice is rescinded as a result of the appeal; but

(c) subject to paragraph (b) above and section 22(4) and (6)(a) below, as from the withdrawal or final determination of the appeal shall be enforceable as if paragraph (a) above had not had effect.

(8) Any sums received by the Secretary of State by virtue of this section shall be paid into the Consolidated Fund.

22. – (1) A person on whom a penalty notice is served may appeal against the notice before the end of the period of four weeks following the date of service of the notice.

> *S.22 - A penalty notice will not be enforceable where the employer has appealed against an enforcement notice until the appeal has been finally determined or withdrawn. An employer has a right of appeal against a penalty notice exercisable within four weeks of receiving it. The penalty notice will not be enforced pending the appeal. The appeal may be heard by a Tribunal Chairman sitting alone. The Tribunal will rescind the penalty notice if the appeal is successful, correct the notice if it is partially successful or dismiss the appeal. To succeed, the employer must show that the enforcement officer has no reason to serve any penalty notice; or that some of the details affecting the amount of the fine given in the notice was incorrect; or that the amount of the fine has been miscalculated*

(2) An appeal under subsection (1) above lies to an employment tribunal.

(3) On an appeal under subsection (1) above, the employment tribunal shall dismiss the appeal unless it is shown-

    (a) that, in the case of each of the allegations of failure to comply with the enforcement notice, the facts are such that an officer who was aware of them would have had no reason to serve any penalty notice on the appellant; or

    (b) that the penalty notice is incorrect in some of the particulars which affect the amount of the financial penalty; or

    (c) that the calculation of the amount of the financial penalty is incorrect;

and for the purposes of any appeal relating to a penalty notice, the enforcement notice in question shall (subject to rescission or rectification on any appeal brought under section 19 above) be taken to be correct.

(4) Where an appeal is allowed by virtue of paragraph (a) of subsection (3) above, the employment tribunal shall rescind the penalty notice.

(5) If, in a case where subsection (4) above does not apply, an appeal is allowed by virtue of paragraph (b) or (c) of subsection (3) above-

    (a) the employment tribunal shall rectify the penalty notice; and

    (b) the penalty notice shall have effect as if it had originally been served as so rectified.

(6) Where a person has appealed under subsection (1) above against a penalty notice and the appeal has not been withdrawn or finally determined, the penalty notice-

    (a) shall not be enforceable until the appeal has been withdrawn or finally determined; but

    (b) subject to subsection (4) above and section 21(7)(a) and (b) above, as from the withdrawal or final determination of the appeal shall be enforceable as if paragraph (a) above had not had effect.

Rights not to suffer unfair dismissal or other detriment

23. – (1) A worker has the right not to be subjected to any detriment by any act, or any deliberate failure to act, by his employer, done on the ground that-

> *S.23 - Workers have the right from the outset of their employment not to be subjected to any detriment by their employer because they have asserted in good faith their right to the NMW, the right of access to records, or their right to recover the difference between what they have been paid and the NMW; or as a result of such assertion, the employer was prosecuted for an offence under the Act; or they qualify, or will or might qualify, for the NMW or for a higher rate of NMW. This section does not apply where the detriment in question amounts to dismissal (except in the specified circumstances) because the protection against dismissal is contained in s.25*

(a) any action was taken, or was proposed to be taken, by or on behalf of the worker with a view to enforcing, or otherwise securing the benefit of, a right of the worker's to which this section applies; or

(b) the employer was prosecuted for an offence under section 31 below as a result of action taken by or on behalf of the worker for the purpose of enforcing, or otherwise securing the benefit of, a right of the worker's to which this section applies; or

(c) the worker qualifies, or will or might qualify, for the national minimum wage or for a particular rate of national minimum wage.

(2) It is immaterial for the purposes of paragraph (a) or (b) of subsection (1) above-

(a) whether or not the worker has the right, or

(b) whether or not the right has been infringed,

but, for that subsection to apply, the claim to the right and, if applicable, the claim that it has been infringed must be made in good faith.

(3) The following are the rights to which this section applies-

(a) any right conferred by, or by virtue of, any provision of this Act for which the remedy for its infringement is by way of a complaint to an employment tribunal; and

(b) any right conferred by section 17 above.

(4) Except where a person is dismissed in circumstances in which-

(a) by virtue of section 197 of the Employment Rights Act 1996 (fixed term contracts), Part X of that Act (unfair dismissal) does not apply to the dismissal, or

(b) in relation to Northern Ireland, by virtue of Article 240 of the Employment Rights (Northern Ireland) Order 1996, Part XI of that Order does not apply to the dismissal, this section does not apply where the detriment in question amounts to dismissal within the meaning of that Part.

24.– (1) A worker may present a complaint to an employment tribunal that he has been subjected to a detriment in contravention of section 23 above.

> **S.24** – *The Employment Tribunal has jurisdiction to deal with a complaint under s.23 that a worker has been subjected to an unlawful detriment*

(2) Subject to the following provisions of this section, the provisions of-

    (a) sections 48(2) to (4) and 49 of the (1996 c. 18.)Employment Rights Act 1996 (complaints to employment tribunals and remedies), or

    (b) in relation to Northern Ireland, Articles 71(2) to (4) and 72 of the (S.I. 1996/1919 (N.I.16).)Employment Rights (Northern Ireland) Order 1996 (complaints to industrial tribunals and remedies),

shall apply in relation to a complaint under this section as they apply in relation to a complaint under section 48 of that Act or Article 71 of that Order (as the case may be), but taking references in those provisions to the employer as references to the employer within the meaning of section 23(1) above.

(3) Where-

    (a) the detriment to which the worker is subjected is the termination of his worker's contract, but

    (b) that contract is not a contract of employment,

any compensation awarded under section 49 of the (1996 c. 18.)Employment Rights Act 1996 or Article 72 of the (S.I. 1996/1919 (N.I.16).)Employment Rights (Northern Ireland) Order 1996 by virtue of subsection (2) above must not exceed the limit specified in subsection (4) below.

(4) The limit mentioned in subsection (3) above is the total of-

    (a) the sum which would be the basic award for unfair dismissal, calculated in accordance with section 119 of the (1996 c. 18.)Employment Rights Act 1996 or Article 153 of the (S.I. 1996/1919 (N.I.16).)Employment Rights (Northern Ireland) Order 1996 (as the case may be), if the worker had been an employee and the contract terminated had been a contract of employment; and

    (b) the sum for the time being specified in section 124(1) of that Act or Article 158(1) of that Order (as the case may be) which is the limit for a compensatory award to a person calculated in accordance with section 123 of that Act or Article 157 of that Order (as the case may be).

(5) Where the worker has been working under arrangements which do not fall to be regarded as a worker's contract for the purposes of-

(a) the Employment Rights Act 1996, or

(b) in relation to Northern Ireland, the Employment Rights (Northern Ireland) Order 1996,

he shall be treated for the purposes of subsections (3) and (4) above as if any arrangements under which he has been working constituted a worker's contract falling within section 230(3)(b) of that Act or Article 3(3)(b) of that Order (as the case may be).

25. – (1) After section 104 of the (1996 c. 18.)Employment Rights Act 1996 (assertion of statutory right) there shall be inserted-

"104A.– (1) An employee who is dismissed shall be regarded for the purposes of this Part as unfairly dismissed if the reason (or, if more than one, the principal reason) for the dismissal is that-

S.25 - A new s.104A and a new s.105(7A) are introduced into the Employment Rights Act 1996. These sections provide that employees (note s.24 refers to "workers") who are dismissed or selected for redundancy will be regarded as automatically unfairly dismissed if the sole or main reason for their dismissal or selection was that they asserted any of the rights referred to in s.23 above; or as a result of such assertion, their employer was prosecuted for an offence under the Act; or they qualify or will or might qualify for the NMW or for a particular NMW rate. The employee gains protection against unfair dismissal immediately without having to work the qualifying period of one year's continuous service and the protection is not lost on reaching the upper age limit in s.109 of the Employment Rights Act 1996

(a) any action was taken, or was proposed to be taken, by or on behalf of the employee with a view to enforcing, or otherwise securing the benefit of, a right of the employee's to which this section applies; or

(b) the employer was prosecuted for an offence under section 31 of the National Minimum Wage Act 1998 as a result of action taken by or on behalf of the employee for the purpose of enforcing, or otherwise securing the benefit of, a right of the employee's to which this section applies; or

(c) the employee qualifies, or will or might qualify, for the national minimum wage or for a particular rate of national minimum wage.

(2) It is immaterial for the purposes of paragraph (a) or (b) of subsection (1) above-

(a) whether or not the employee has the right, or

(b) whether or not the right has been infringed,

but, for that subsection to apply, the claim to the right and, if applicable, the claim that it has been infringed must be made in good faith.

(3) The following are the rights to which this section applies-

    (a) any right conferred by, or by virtue of, any provision of the National Minimum Wage Act 1998 for which the remedy for its infringement is by way of a complaint to an employment tribunal; and

    (b) any right conferred by section 17 of the National Minimum Wage Act 1998 (worker receiving less than national minimum wage entitled to additional remuneration)."

(2) In section 105 of that Act (redundancy as unfair dismissal) in subsection (1)(c) (which refers to any of subsections (2) to (7) of that section applying) for "(7)" there shall be substituted "(7A)" and after subsection (7) there shall be inserted-

"(7A) This subsection applies if the reason (or, if more than one, the principal reason) for which the employee was selected for dismissal was one of those specified in subsection (1) of section 104A (read with subsection (2) of that section)."

(3) In section 108 of that Act (exclusion of right: qualifying period of employment) in subsection (3) (cases where no qualifying period is required) the word "or" at the end of paragraph (g) shall be omitted and after that paragraph there shall be inserted-

"(gg) subsection (1) of section 104A (read with subsection (2) of that section) applies, or".

(4) In section 109 of that Act (exclusion of right: upper age limit) in subsection (2) (cases where upper age limit does not apply) the word "or" at the end of paragraph (g) shall be omitted and after that paragraph there shall be inserted-

"(gg) subsection (1) of section 104A (read with subsection (2) of that section) applies, or".

26. – (1) After Article 135 of the Employment Rights (Northern Ireland) Order 1996 (assertion of statutory right) there shall be inserted-

"The national minimum wage.

    135A. – (1) An employee who is dismissed shall be regarded for the purposes of this Part as unfairly dismissed if the reason (or, if more than one, the principal reason) for the dismissal is that-

> *S.26 - Protection against unfair dismissal for employees in Northern Ireland, comparable to the protection for employees in Great Britain under s.25, are provided by new provisions in the Employment Rights (Northern Ireland) Order 1996*

    (a) any action was taken, or was proposed to be taken, by or on behalf of the employee with a view to enforcing, or otherwise securing the benefit of, a right of the employee's to which this Article applies; or

(b) the employer was prosecuted for an offence under section 31 of the National Minimum Wage Act 1998 as a result of action taken by or on behalf of the employee for the purpose of enforcing, or otherwise securing the benefit of, a right of the employee's to which this Article applies; or

(c) the employee qualifies, or will or might qualify, for the national minimum wage or for a particular rate of national minimum wage.

(2) It is immaterial for the purposes of sub-paragraph (a) or (b) of paragraph (1)-

(a) whether or not the employee has the right, or

(b) whether or not the right has been infringed;

but, for that paragraph to apply, the claim to the right and, if applicable, the claim that it has been infringed must be made in good faith.

(3) The following are the rights to which this Article applies-

(a) any right conferred by, or by virtue of, any provision of the National Minimum Wage Act 1998 for which the remedy for its infringement is by way of a complaint to an industrial tribunal, and

(b) any right conferred by section 17 of the National Minimum Wage Act 1998 (worker receiving less than national minimum wage entitled to additional remuneration)."

(2) In Article 137 of that Order (redundancy as unfair dismissal) after paragraph (6) there shall be inserted-

"(6A) This paragraph applies if the reason (or, if more than one, the principal reason) for which the employee was selected for dismissal was one of those specified in paragraph (1) of Article 135A (read with paragraph (2) of that Article)."

(3) In Article 140 of that Order (exclusion of right: qualifying period of employment) in paragraph (3) (cases where no qualifying period is required) after sub-paragraph (f) there shall be inserted-

"(ff) paragraph (1) of Article 135A (read with paragraph (2) of that Article) applies,".

(4) In Article 141 of that Order (exclusion of right: upper age limit) in paragraph (2) (cases where upper age limit does not apply) after sub-paragraph (f) there shall be inserted-

"(ff) paragraph (1) of Article 135A (read with paragraph (2) of that Article) applies,".

(5) In Article 142 of that Order (exclusion of right: dismissal procedures agreements) in paragraph (2) (cases where paragraph (1) does not apply) the word "or" at the end of sub-paragraph (b) shall be omitted and after sub-paragraph (c) there shall be added "or

(d) paragraph (1) of Article 135A (read with paragraph (2) of that Article) applies."

(6) The Department of Economic Development may by order repeal subsection (5) above and this subsection.

Civil procedure, evidence and appeals

27. – (1) In section 4 of the Employment Tribunals Act 1996 (composition of employment tribunal) in subsection (3) (which specifies proceedings to be heard by the chairman alone) after paragraph (ca) there shall be inserted-

> *S.27 - S.4 of the Employment Tribunals Act 1996 (composition of Employment Tribunals) is amended to provide for a Chairman alone to determine complaints under s.11 and appeals under s.19 and s.22 of the Act. There are comparable provisions amending Article 6 of the Industrial Tribunals (Northern Ireland) Order 1996*

"(cc) proceedings on a complaint under section 11 of the National Minimum Wage Act 1998;

(cd) proceedings on an appeal under section 19 or 22 of the National Minimum Wage Act 1998;".

(2) In Article 6 of the Industrial Tribunals (Northern Ireland) Order 1996 (composition of industrial tribunal in Northern Ireland) in paragraph (3) (which specifies proceedings to be heard by the chairman alone) after sub-paragraph (b) there shall be inserted-

"(bb) proceedings on a complaint under section 11 of the National Minimum Wage Act 1998;

(bc) proceedings on an appeal under section 19 or 22 of the National Minimum Wage Act 1998;".

28. – (1) Where in any civil proceedings any question arises as to whether an individual qualifies or qualified at any time for the national minimum wage, it shall be presumed that the individual qualifies or, as the case may be, qualified at that time for the national minimum wage unless the contrary is established.

> *S.28 - Where a person claiming to have been paid less than the NMW presents a complaint to an Employment Tribunal or institutes civil proceedings in order to recover the underpayment, there will be a presumption that the Applicant qualifies for the NMW and was paid below the NMW. Accordingly the onus to prove compliance will be on the employer, if the Applicant's complaint is disputed*

(2) Where-

    (a) a complaint is made-

        (i) to an employment tribunal under section 23(1)(a) of the Employment Rights Act 1996 (unauthorised deductions from wages), or

        (ii) to an industrial tribunal under Article 55(1)(a) of the Employment Rights (Northern Ireland) Order 1996, and

    (b) the complaint relates in whole or in part to the deduction of the amount described as additional remuneration in section 17(1) above,

it shall be presumed for the purposes of the complaint, so far as relating to the deduction of that amount, that the worker in question was remunerated at a rate less than the national minimum wage unless the contrary is established.

(3) Where in any civil proceedings a person seeks to recover on a claim in contract the amount described as additional remuneration in section 17(1) above, it shall be presumed for the purposes of the proceedings, so far as relating to that amount, that the worker in question was remunerated at a rate less than the national minimum wage unless the contrary is established.

29. In section 21(1) of the Employment Tribunals Act 1996 (appeal from employment tribunal to Employment Appeal Tribunal on question of law arising under or by virtue of the enactments there specified) after paragraph (f) there shall be inserted-

> **S.29** - *Appeals from decisions of Employment Tribunals will lie to the Employment Appeal Tribunal*

"(ff) the National Minimum Wage Act 1998, or".

Conciliation

30. – (1) In section 18 of the Employment Tribunals Act 1996 (conciliation) in subsection (1) (which specifies the proceedings and claims to which the section applies) after paragraph (d) there shall be inserted-

> **S.30** - *ACAS conciliation officers may conciliate complaints presented to Employment Tribunals under the Act*

"(dd) under or by virtue of section 11, 18, 20(1)(a) or 24 of the National Minimum Wage Act 1998;".

(2) In Article 20 of the (S.I. 1996/1921 (N.I.18).)Industrial Tribunals (Northern Ireland) Order 1996 (conciliation) in paragraph (1) (which specifies the

proceedings and claims to which the Article applies) after sub-paragraph (c) there shall be inserted-

"(cc) under or by virtue of section 11, 18, 20(1)(b) or 24 of the National Minimum Wage Act 1998;".

Offences

31. – (1) If the employer of a worker who qualifies for the national minimum wage refuses or wilfully neglects to remunerate the worker for any pay reference period at a rate which is at least equal to the national minimum wage, that employer is guilty of an offence.

> *S.31 - It is a criminal offence for an employer to refuse or wilfully neglect to pay a worker an hourly rate at least equal to the NMW; knowingly to keep false records; knowingly to produce or furnish false records or other information; intentionally to delay or obstruct an enforcement officer; and to refuse or to neglect to answer a question, furnish information or produce a document when required to do so by an enforcement officer. The offences are triable before Magistrates. The maximum penalty for each offence is a fine not exceeding level 5 on the standard scale, currently, £5,000. It is a defence if the employer proves that it exercised all due diligence and took all reasonable precautions to secure that it complied with the Act or the Regulations*

(2) If a person who is required to keep or preserve any record in accordance with regulations under section 9 above fails to do so, that person is guilty of an offence.

(3) If a person makes, or knowingly causes or allows to be made, in a record required to be kept in accordance with regulations under section 9 above any entry which he knows to be false in a material particular, that person is guilty of an offence.

(4) If a person, for purposes connected with the provisions of this Act, produces or furnishes, or knowingly causes or allows to be produced or furnished, any record or information which he knows to be false in a material particular, that person is guilty of an offence.

(5) If a person-

    (a) intentionally delays or obstructs an officer acting for the purposes of this Act in the exercise of any power conferred by this Act, or

    (b) refuses or neglects to answer any question, furnish any information or produce any document when required to do so under section 14(1) above,

that person is guilty of an offence.

(6) Where the commission by any person of an offence under subsection (1) or (2) above is due to the act or default of some other person, that other person is also guilty of the offence.

(7) A person may be charged with and convicted of an offence by virtue of subsection (6) above whether or not proceedings are taken against any other person.

(8) In any proceedings for an offence under subsection (1) or (2) above it shall be a defence for the person charged to prove that he exercised all due diligence and took all reasonable precautions to secure that the provisions of this Act, and of any relevant regulations made under it, were complied with by himself and by any person under his control.

(9) A person guilty of an offence under this section shall be liable on summary conviction to a fine not exceeding level 5 on the standard scale.

32. – (1) This section applies to any offence under this Act.

> *S.32 - Where the employer is a company or other corporate body, a director manager secretary or other similar officer of the body or a person purporting to act in any such capacity will be held jointly responsible with the company or corporate body for offences under s.31 where they are proved to have been committed with their consent or connivance, or to be attributable to any neglect on their part. This applies to the members of a management company and the partners in a partnership in Scotland*

(2) If an offence committed by a body corporate is proved-

    (a) to have been committed with the consent or connivance of an officer of the body, or

    (b) to be attributable to any neglect on the part of such an officer,

the officer as well as the body corporate is guilty of the offence and liable to be proceeded against and punished accordingly.

(3) In subsection (2) above "officer", in relation to a body corporate, means a director, manager, secretary or other similar officer of the body, or a person purporting to act in any such capacity.

(4) If the affairs of a body corporate are managed by its members, subsection (2) above applies in relation to the acts and defaults of a member in connection with his functions of management as if he were a director of the body corporate.

(5) If an offence committed by a partnership in Scotland is proved-

    (a) to have been committed with the consent or connivance of a partner, or

    (b) to be attributable to any neglect on the part of a partner, the partner as well as the partnership is guilty of the offence and liable to be proceeded against and punished accordingly.

(6) In subsection (5) above, "partner" includes a person purporting to act as a partner.

Proceedings for offences.

33. – (1) The persons who may conduct proceedings for an offence under this Act-

> **S.33** - *The Secretary of State can authorise enforcement officers or other non-lawyers to prosecute offences under s.31 in the Magistrates Courts in England and Wales or in a Court of Summary Jurisdiction in Northern Ireland, within time limits for bringing prosecutions in those jurisdictions and in Scotland*

    (a) in England and Wales, before a magistrates' court, or

    (b) in Northern Ireland, before a court of summary jurisdiction,

shall include any person authorised for the purpose by the Secretary of State even if that person is not a barrister or solicitor.

(2) In England and Wales or Northern Ireland, proceedings for an offence under this Act may be begun at any time within whichever of the following periods expires the later, that is to say-

    (a) the period of 6 months from the date on which evidence, sufficient in the opinion of the Secretary of State to justify a prosecution for the offence, comes to the knowledge of the Secretary of State, or

    (b) the period of 12 months from the commission of the offence,

notwithstanding anything in any other enactment (including an enactment comprised in Northern Ireland legislation) or in any instrument made under an enactment.

(3) For the purposes of subsection (2) above, a certificate purporting to be signed by or on behalf of the Secretary of State as to the date on which such evidence as is mentioned in paragraph (a) of that subsection came to the knowledge of the Secretary of State shall be conclusive evidence of that date.

(4) In Scotland, proceedings for an offence under this Act may, notwithstanding anything in section 136 of the (1995 c. 46.)Criminal Procedure (Scotland) Act 1995, be commenced at any time within-

    (a) the period of 6 months from the date on which evidence, sufficient in the opinion of the procurator fiscal to justify proceedings, comes to the knowledge of the procurator fiscal, or

    (b) the period of 12 months from the commission of the offence,

whichever period expires the later.

(5) For the purposes of subsection (4) above-

    (a) a certificate purporting to be signed by or on behalf of the procurator fiscal as to the date on which such evidence as is mentioned above came to the knowledge of the procurator fiscal shall be conclusive evidence of that date; and

    (b) subsection (3) of section 136 of the said Act of 1995 (date of commencement of proceedings) shall have effect as it has effect for the purposes of that section.

Special classes of person

Agency workers who are not otherwise "workers".

34. – (1) This section applies in any case where an individual ("the agency worker")-

    (a) is supplied by a person ("the agent") to do work for another ("the principal") under a contract or other arrangements made between the agent and the principal; but

> *S.34 - The Act applies to an "agency worker" who would not otherwise be a "worker" within the meaning of the Act because although the form of relationship they have involves working for a remuneration, the statutory definition of "worker" is not met. S.34 applies the Act as if the agency worker has a contract with the person responsible for paying him or her or, if neither the agent nor the person or business that hires him or her is responsible for payment, with which ever of them actually pays him or her. This should prove to be an effective anti-avoidance measure for those who seek to establish complex work relationships to defeat the NMW provisions*

    (b) is not, as respects that work, a worker, because of the absence of a worker's contract between the individual and the agent or the principal; and

    (c) is not a party to a contract under which he undertakes to do the work for another party to the contract whose status is, by virtue of the contract, that of a client or customer of any profession or business undertaking carried on by the individual.

(2) In a case where this section applies, the other provisions of this Act shall have effect as if there were a worker's contract for the doing of the work by the agency worker made between the agency worker and-

    (a) whichever of the agent and the principal is responsible for paying the agency worker in respect of the work; or

    (b) if neither the agent nor the principal is so responsible, whichever of them pays the agency worker in respect of the work.

Home workers who are not otherwise "workers".

35. – (1) In determining for the purposes of this Act whether a home worker is or is not a worker, section 54(3)(b) below shall have effect as if for the word "personally" there were substituted "(whether personally or otherwise)".

> **S.35** - *"Home work" is widely defined as applying when an individual enters into a contract with a person, for the purposes of that person's business, to carry out work in a place not under the control or management of that person. It need not necessarily therefore be at the home worker's home. S.54(3)(b) is modified in connection with a home worker to remove the requirement that the worker undertakes the work personally, in order to provide coverage where the home worker delegates or is assisted by family members or others*

(2) In this section "home worker" means an individual who contracts with a person, for the purposes of that person's business, for the execution of work to be done in a place not under the control or management of that person.

Crown employment.

36. – (1) Subject to section 37 below, the provisions of this Act have effect in relation to Crown employment and persons in Crown employment as they have effect in relation to other employment and other workers.

> **S.36** - *The Act is applied to those in Crown employment, subject to s.37 and the definition of Crown employment. The definition will include civilian workers in Crown employment*

(2) In this Act, subject to section 37 below, "Crown employment" means employment under or for the purposes of a government department or any officer or body exercising on behalf of the Crown functions conferred by statutory provision.

(3) For the purposes of the application of the other provisions of this Act in relation to Crown employment in accordance with subsection (1) above-

(a) references to an employee or a worker shall be construed as references to a person in Crown employment;

(b) references to a contract of employment or a worker's contract shall be construed as references to the terms of employment of a person in Crown employment; and

(c) references to dismissal, or to the termination of a worker's contract, shall be construed as references to the termination of Crown employment.

37. – (1) A person serving as a member of the naval, military or air forces of the Crown does not qualify for the national minimum wage in respect of that service.

> *S.37 - The Act does not apply to a person serving as a member of the Navy, Army or Royal Air Force but does apply to employment by an association established under Part XI of the Reserve Forces Act 1996*

(2) Section 36 above applies to employment by an association established for the purposes of Part XI of the Reserve Forces Act 1996, notwithstanding anything in subsection (1) above.

38. – (1) Apart from section 21 above, the provisions of this Act have effect in relation to employment as a relevant member of the House of Lords staff as they have effect in relation to other employment.

> *S.38 - The Act applies to a member of the House of Lords staff and expressly confirms the right to bring a claim under the Act before a civil court*

(2) Nothing in any rule of law or the law or practice of Parliament prevents a relevant member of the House of Lords staff from bringing before the High Court or a county court any claim under this Act.

(3) In this section "relevant member of the House of Lords staff" means any person who is employed under a worker's contract with the Corporate Officer of the House of Lords.

39. – (1) Apart from section 21 above, the provisions of this Act have effect in relation to employment as a relevant member of the House of Commons staff as they have effect in relation to other employment.

> *S.39 - The Act applies to a member of the House of Commons staff or a member of the Speaker's personal staff and expressly confirms the right to bring a claim under the Act before a civil court*

(2) Nothing in any rule of law or the law or practice of Parliament prevents a relevant member of the House of Commons staff from bringing before the High Court or a county court any claim under this Act.

(3) In this section "relevant member of the House of Commons staff" means any person-

(a) who was appointed by the House of Commons Commission; or
(b) who is a member of the Speaker's personal staff.

40. For the purposes of this Act, an individual employed to work on board a ship registered in the United Kingdom under Part II of the Merchant Shipping Act 1995 shall be treated as an individual who under his contract ordinarily works in the United Kingdom unless-

> *S.40 - The Act applies to those employed to work on board a UK-registered ship unless the employment is wholly outside the United Kingdom or the person is not ordinarily resident in the United Kingdom*

(a) the employment is wholly outside the United Kingdom; or
(b) the person is not ordinarily resident in the United Kingdom;

and related expressions shall be construed accordingly.

Extensions

41. The Secretary of State may by regulations make provision for this Act to apply, with or without modifications, as if-

> *S.41 - The Secretary of State may make Regulations to apply the Act to individuals who do not otherwise meet the definition of a "worker" – No regulations have been made at the date of publication*

(a) any individual of a prescribed description who would not otherwise be a worker for the purposes of this Act were a worker for those purposes;
(b) there were in the case of any such individual a worker's contract of a prescribed description under which the individual works; and
(c) a person of a prescribed description were the employer under that contract.

42. – (1) In this section "offshore employment" means employment for the purposes of activities-

S.42 - *The Act may be applied to those in offshore employment by an Order in Council. The definition in s.201(1) of the Employment Rights Act 1996 is adopted. The National Minimum Wage (Offshore Employment) Order 1999 extends the provisions of the Act and regulations to British and foreign workers who work in United Kingdom territorial waters or in certain circumstances in the UK or foreign sector of the continental shelf, mainly work on oil or gas rigs*

    (a) in the territorial waters of the United Kingdom, or

    (b) connected with the exploration of the sea-bed or subsoil, or the exploitation of their natural resources, in the United Kingdom sector of the continental shelf, or

    (c) connected with the exploration or exploitation, in a foreign sector of the continental shelf, of a cross-boundary petroleum field.

(2) Her Majesty may by Order in Council provide that the provisions of this Act apply, to such extent and for such purposes as may be specified in the Order (with or without modification), to or in relation to a person in offshore employment.

(3) An Order in Council under this section-

    (a) may provide that all or any of the provisions of this Act, as applied by such an Order in Council, apply-

        (i) to individuals whether or not they are British subjects, and

        (ii) to bodies corporate whether or not they are incorporated under the law of a part of the United Kingdom,

and apply even where the application may affect their activities outside the United Kingdom,

    (b) may make provision for conferring jurisdiction on any court or class of court specified in the Order in Council, or on employment tribunals, in respect of offences, causes of action or other matters arising in connection with offshore employment,

    (c) may (without prejudice to subsection (2) above) provide that the provisions of this Act, as applied by the Order in Council, apply in relation to any person in employment in a part of the areas referred to in subsection (1)(a) and (b) above,

    (d) may exclude from the operation of section 3 of the Territorial Waters Jurisdiction Act 1878 (consents required for prosecutions) proceedings for offences under this Act in connection with offshore employment,

    (e) may provide that such proceedings shall not be brought without such consent as may be required by the Order in Council,

    (f) may (without prejudice to subsection (2) above) modify or exclude the operation of sections 1(2)(b) and 40 above.

(4) Any jurisdiction conferred on a court or tribunal under this section is without prejudice to jurisdiction exercisable apart from this section by that or any other court or tribunal.

(5) In this section-

"cross-boundary petroleum field" means a petroleum field that extends across the boundary between the United Kingdom sector of the continental shelf and a foreign sector of the continental shelf,

"foreign sector of the continental shelf" means an area outside the territorial waters of any state, within which rights with respect to the sea-bed and subsoil and their natural resources are exercisable by a state other than the United Kingdom,

"petroleum field" means a geological structure identified as an oil or gas field by the Order in Council concerned, and

"United Kingdom sector of the continental shelf" means the area designated under section 1(7) of the Continental Shelf Act 1964.

Exclusions

43. A person-

> *S.43 - A share fisherman, i.e. a person employed as master, or as a member of the crew, of a fishing vessel, and remunerated in respect of that employment, only by a share in the profits or gross earnings of the vessel is excluded from the protection of the Act*

(a) employed as master, or as a member of the crew, of a fishing vessel, and
(b) remunerated, in respect of that employment, only by a share in the profits or gross earnings of the vessel,

does not qualify for the national minimum wage in respect of that employment.

44. – (1) A worker employed by a charity, a voluntary organisation, an associated fund-raising body or a statutory body does not qualify for the national minimum wage in respect of that employment if he receives, and under the terms of his employment (apart from this Act) is entitled to,-

> **S.44** - *Voluntary workers who are employed by charities, voluntary organisations, bodies separate from those organisations but whose profits go to them (such as a body operating a charity shop) or statutory bodies (such as schools or hospitals), do not qualify for the NMW if they are unpaid or only receive actual or reasonably estimated travel or out of pocket expenses; receive no benefits in kind or none except "reasonable" subsistence or accommodation or training which is geared to improving their ability to perform the work; and where they have been placed with their employer by a charity such as Community Service volunteers, receive a subsistence allowance*

(a) no monetary payments of any description, or no monetary payments except in respect of expenses-
   (i) actually incurred in the performance of his duties; or
   (ii) reasonably estimated as likely to be or to have been so incurred; and
(b) no benefits in kind of any description, or no benefits in kind other than the provision of some or all of his subsistence or of such accommodation as is reasonable in the circumstances of the employment.

(2) A person who would satisfy the conditions in subsection (1) above but for receiving monetary payments made solely for the purpose of providing him with means of subsistence shall be taken to satisfy those conditions if-

(a) he is employed to do the work in question as a result of arrangements made between a charity acting in pursuance of its charitable purposes and the body for which the work is done; and
(b) the work is done for a charity, a voluntary organisation, an associated fund-raising body or a statutory body.

(3) For the purposes of subsection (1)(b) above-

(a) any training (other than that which a person necessarily acquires in the course of doing his work) shall be taken to be a benefit in kind; but
(b) there shall be left out of account any training provided for the sole or main purpose of improving the worker's ability to perform the work which he has agreed to do.

(4) In this section-

"associated fund-raising body" means a body of persons the profits of which are applied wholly for the purposes of a charity or voluntary organisation;

"charity" means a body of persons, or the trustees of a trust, established for charitable purposes only;

"receive", in relation to a monetary payment or a benefit in kind, means receive in respect of, or otherwise in connection with, the employment in question (whether or not under the terms of the employment);

"statutory body" means a body established by or under an enactment (including an enactment comprised in Northern Ireland legislation);

"subsistence" means such subsistence as is reasonable in the circumstances of the employment in question, and does not include accommodation;

"voluntary organisation" means a body of persons, or the trustees of a trust, which is established only for charitable purposes (whether or not those purposes are charitable within the meaning of any rule of law), benevolent purposes or philanthropic purposes, but which is not a charity.

45. – (1) A prisoner does not qualify for the national minimum wage in respect of any work which he does in pursuance of prison rules.

(2) In this section-

"prisoner" means a person detained in, or on temporary release from, a prison;

S.45 - Prisoners in custody, including those on remand, working under Prison rules are excluded from the Act

"prison" includes any other institution to which prison rules apply;

"prison rules" means-

(a) in relation to England and Wales, rules made under section 47 of the Prison Act 1952;

(b) in relation to Scotland, rules made under section 39 of the Prisons (Scotland) Act 1989; and

(c) in relation to Northern Ireland, rules made under section 13 of the Prison Act Northern Ireland) 1953.

Agricultural workers

46. – (1) A person who has been prosecuted for an offence which falls within paragraph (a) or (b) below, that is to say-

S.46 - The Act applies the NMW to agricultural workers and the NMW will constitute the minimum hourly rate below which the pay of agricultural workers must not fall. The Agricultural Wages Schemes in England and Wales, Scotland and Northern Ireland and the Agricultural Wages Board will continue, with the powers of the Boards to set minimum conditions for agricultural workers. The Agricultural Wages legislation is amended by Schedule 2 to the Act

(a) an offence under any provision of this Act in its application for the purposes of the agricultural wages legislation, or

(b) an offence under any provision of this Act in its application otherwise than for the purposes of the agricultural wages legislation,

shall not also be liable to be prosecuted for an offence which falls within the other of those paragraphs but which is constituted by the same conduct or alleged conduct for which he was prosecuted.

(2) No amount shall be recoverable both-

(a) under or by virtue of this Act in its application for the purposes of the agricultural wages legislation, and

(b) under or by virtue of this Act in its application otherwise than for those purposes,

in respect of the same work.

(3) Nothing in the agricultural wages legislation, or in any order under that legislation, affects the operation of this Act in its application otherwise than for the purposes of that legislation.

(4) In this section "the agricultural wages legislation" means-

(a) the Agricultural Wages Act 1948;

(b) the Agricultural Wages (Scotland) Act 1949; and

(c) the Agricultural Wages (Regulation) (Northern Ireland) Order 1977.

47. – (1) The following enactments, that is to say-

> **S.47** – *This section provides for the amendments in Schedule 2 regarding statutory provisions affecting agricultural workers*

(a) the Agricultural Wages Act 1948,

(b) the Agricultural Wages (Scotland) Act 1949, and

(c) the Agricultural Wages (Regulation) (Northern Ireland) Order 1977,

shall be amended in accordance with Schedule 2 to this Act.

(2) The appropriate authority may by regulations amend-

(a) the Agricultural Wages Act 1948;

(b) the Agricultural Wages (Scotland) Act 1949;

(c) section 67 of the Agriculture Act 1967 (sick pay);

(d) section 46 of the Agriculture (Miscellaneous Provisions) Act 1968 (further functions of agricultural wages committees); and

(e) the Agricultural Wages (Regulation) (Northern Ireland) Order 1977.

(3) The amendments that may be made under subsection (2) above are any amendments which are consequential on this Act or on regulations under section 1(4), 2 or 3 above.

(4) The appropriate authority may by regulations amend, or make provision in substitution for,-

   (a) section 7 of the (1948 c. 47.)Agricultural Wages Act 1948 (reckoning of benefits and advantages as payment of wages);
   (b) section 7 of the (1949 c. 30.)Agricultural Wages (Scotland) Act 1949 (similar provision for Scotland); or
   (c) Article 4(3) and (5) of the (S.I. 1977/2151 (N.I.22).)Agricultural Wages (Regulation) (Northern Ireland) Order 1977.

(5) Subsection (1) above is without prejudice to subsections (2) to (4) above.

(6) In this section "the appropriate authority" means-

   (a) in relation to England and Wales, the Secretary of State and the Minister of Agriculture, Fisheries and Food acting jointly;
   (b) in relation to Scotland, the Secretary of State;
   (c) in relation to Northern Ireland, the Department of Agriculture for Northern Ireland.

Miscellaneous

48. Where-

> **S.48** - *Where the worker's employer is himself in the employment of some third party, and the worker is employed on the premises of the third party, the third party is treated for the purposes of the Act as jointly liable with the employer. The arrangement where there is a "superior employer" arises in some sectors e.g. "gangmasters" and farmers in agriculture and in the building industry*

   (a) the immediate employer of a worker is himself in the employment of some other person, and
   (b) the worker is employed on the premises of that other person,

that other person shall be deemed for the purposes of this Act to be the employer of the worker jointly with the immediate employer.

49.– (1) Any provision in any agreement (whether a worker's contract or not) is void in so far as it purports-

> **S.49** - *Any agreement which seeks to exclude or limit the operation of the Act's provisions or to preclude a person from complaining to an Employment Tribunal is void except where an ACAS conciliation officer has conciliated the complaint or an agreement satisfying the statutory requirements for compromise agreements have been reached*

    (a) to exclude or limit the operation of any provision of this Act; or

    (b) to preclude a person from bringing proceedings under this Act before an employment tribunal.

(2) Subsection (1) above does not apply to any agreement to refrain from instituting or continuing proceedings where a conciliation officer has taken action under-

    (a) section 18 of the Employment Tribunals Act 1996 (conciliation), or

    (b) in relation to Northern Ireland, Article 20 of the Industrial Tribunals (Northern Ireland) Order 1996.

(3) Subsection (1) above does not apply to any agreement to refrain from instituting or continuing before an employment tribunal any proceedings within-

    (a) section 18(1)(dd) of the (1996 c. 17.)Employment Tribunals Act 1996 (proceedings under or by virtue of this Act where conciliation is available), or

    (b) in relation to Northern Ireland, Article 20(1)(cc) of the (S.I. 1996/1921 (N.I.18).)Industrial Tribunals (Northern Ireland) Order 1996,

if the conditions regulating compromise agreements under this Act are satisfied in relation to the agreement.

(4) For the purposes of subsection (3) above the conditions regulating compromise agreements under this Act are that-

    (a) the agreement must be in writing,

    (b) the agreement must relate to the particular proceedings,

    (c) the employee or worker must have received advice from a relevant independent adviser as to the terms and effect of the proposed agreement and, in particular, its effect on his ability to pursue his rights before an employment tribunal,

    (d) there must be in force, when the adviser gives the advice, a contract of insurance, or an indemnity provided for members of a profession or a professional body, covering the risk of a claim by the employee or worker in respect of loss arising in consequence of the advice,

    (e) the agreement must identify the adviser, and

    (f) the agreement must state that the conditions regulating compromise agreements under this Act are satisfied.

(5) A person is a relevant independent adviser for the purposes of subsection (4)(c) above-

(a) if he is a qualified lawyer,

(b) if he is an officer, official, employee or member of an independent trade union who has been certified in writing by the trade union as competent to give advice and as authorised to do so on behalf of the trade union,

(c) if he works at an advice centre (whether as an employee or a volunteer) and has been certified in writing by the centre as competent to give advice and as authorised to do so on behalf of the centre, or

(d) if he is a person of a description specified in an order made by the Secretary of State.

(6) But a person is not a relevant independent adviser for the purposes of subsection (4)(c) above in relation to the employee or worker-

(a) if he is employed by, or is acting in the matter for, the employer or an associated employer,

(b) in the case of a person within subsection (5)(b) or (c) above, if the trade union or advice centre is the employer or an associated employer,

(c) in the case of a person within subsection (5)(c) above, if the employee or worker makes a payment for the advice received from him, or

(d) in the case of a person of a description specified in an order under subsection (5)(d) above, if any condition specified in the order in relation to the giving of advice by persons of that description is not satisfied.

(7) In this section "qualified lawyer" means-

(a) as respects England and Wales-
  (i) a barrister (whether in practice as such or employed to give legal advice);
  (ii) a solicitor who holds a practising certificate; or
  (iii) a person other than a barrister or solicitor who is an authorised advocate or authorised litigator (within the meaning of the Courts and Legal Services Act 1990);

(b) as respects Scotland-
  (i) an advocate (whether in practice as such or employed to give legal advice); or
  (ii) a solicitor who holds a practising certificate; and

(c) as respects Northern Ireland-
  (i) a barrister (whether in practice as such or employed to give legal advice); or
  (ii) a solicitor who holds a practising certificate.

(8) For the purposes of this section any two employers shall be treated as associated if-

(a) one is a company of which the other (directly or indirectly) has control; or

(b) both are companies of which a third person (directly or indirectly) has control;

and "associated employer" shall be construed accordingly.

(9) In the application of this section in relation to Northern Ireland-

(a) subsection (4)(c) above shall have effect as if for "advice from a relevant independent adviser" there were substituted "independent legal advice from a qualified lawyer"; and

(b) subsection (4)(d) above shall have effect as if for "contract of insurance, or an indemnity provided for members of a profession or a professional body," there were substituted "policy of insurance".

(10) In subsection (4) above, as it has effect by virtue of subsection (9) above, "independent", in relation to legal advice received by an employee or worker, means that the advice is given by a lawyer who is not acting in the matter for the employer or an associated employer.

(11) The Secretary of State may by order repeal subsections (9) and (10) above and this subsection.

50. – (1) The Secretary of State shall arrange for information about this Act and regulations under it to be published by such means as appear to the Secretary of State to be most appropriate for drawing the provisions of this Act and those regulations to the attention of persons affected by them.

S.50 - The Secretary of State is obliged to publicise the Act and the Regulations by the most appropriate means for drawing the provisions of the Act and Regulations to the attention of persons affected by them i.e. both employers and workers as widely defined by the Act. The publicity must include the hourly rate of the NMW, the method of calculating a person's hourly rate during any pay reference period, the enforcement machinery and information about workers excluded from the Act or having modified rights. Extensive publicity at a cost of £5m has been undertaken together with an impressive range of literature, CD ROM's, illustrative case studies, workshops and seminars. There are also telephone helplines and "freepost" enquiry facilities readily available

(2) The information required to be published under subsection (1) above includes, in particular, information about-

(a) the hourly rate for the time being prescribed under section 1 above;

(b) the method or methods to be used for determining under section 2 above the hourly rate at which a person is to be regarded for the purposes of this Act as remunerated by his employer in respect of his work in any pay reference period;

(c) the methods of enforcing rights under this Act; and

(d) the persons to whom section 3 above applies and the provision made in relation to them by regulations under that section.

Supplementary

51. – (1) Except to the extent that this Act makes provision to the contrary, any power conferred by this Act to make an Order in Council, regulations or an order includes power-

> **S.51** - *Provides for the making of orders and regulations*

   (a) to make different provision for different cases or for different descriptions of person; and

   (b) to make incidental, consequential, supplemental or transitional provision and savings.

(2) Paragraph (a) of subsection (1) above does not have effect in relation to regulations under section 1(3) above or an order under section 49 above.

(3) No recommendation shall be made to Her Majesty to make an Order in Council under any provision of this Act unless a draft of the Order in Council has been laid before Parliament and approved by a resolution of each House of Parliament.

(4) Any power of a Minister of the Crown to make regulations or an order under this Act shall be exercisable by statutory instrument.

(5) A statutory instrument containing (whether alone or with other provisions) regulations under this Act shall not be made unless a draft of the instrument has been laid before, and approved by a resolution of, each House of Parliament.

(6) Subsection (5) above shall not have effect in relation to a statutory instrument if the only regulations under this Act which the instrument contains are regulations under section 21 or 47(2) or (4) above.

(7) A statutory instrument-

   (a) which contains (whether alone or with other provisions) any regulations under section 21 or 47(2) or (4) above or an order under section 49 above, and

   (b) which is not subject to any requirement that a draft of the instrument be laid before, and approved by a resolution of, each House of Parliament,

shall be subject to annulment in pursuance of a resolution of either House of Parliament.

(8) The power-

   (a) of the Department of Economic Development to make an order under section 26(6) above, or

   (b) of the Department of Agriculture for Northern Ireland to make regulations under section 47 above, shall be exercisable by statutory rule for the purposes of the Statutory Rules (Northern Ireland) Order 1979; and any such order or regulations shall be subject to negative resolution within the meaning of section 41(6) of the Interpretation Act Northern Ireland) 1954.

52. There shall be paid out of money provided by Parliament-

> **S.52** - *The funding by Parliament of the expenditure incurred in implementing this Act is authorised*

(a) any expenditure incurred under this Act by a Minister of the Crown or government department or by a body performing functions on behalf of the Crown; and

(b) any increase attributable to the provisions of this Act in the sums payable out of such money under any other Act.

53. The enactments mentioned in Schedule 3 to this Act are repealed, and the instruments mentioned in that Schedule are revoked, to the extent specified in the third column of that Schedule.

> **S.53** - *This provides for repeals and revocations set out in Schedule 3*

54. – (1) In this Act "employee" means an individual who has entered into or works under (or, where the employment has ceased, worked under) a contract of employment.

> **S.54** - *The well established definitions of "employee", "contract of employment", "worker", "employer" and "employment" in s.230(1)-(5) of the Employment Rights Act 1996 are adopted by the Act*

(2) In this Act "contract of employment" means a contract of service or apprenticeship, whether express or implied, and (if it is express) whether oral or in writing.

(3) In this Act "worker" (except in the phrases "agency worker" and "home worker") means an individual who has entered into or works under (or, where the employment has ceased, worked under)-

(a) a contract of employment; or

(b) any other contract, whether express or implied and (if it is express) whether oral or in writing, whereby the individual undertakes to do or perform personally any work or services for another party to the contract whose status is not by virtue of the contract that of a client or customer of any profession or business undertaking carried on by the individual;

and any reference to a worker's contract shall be construed accordingly.

(4) In this Act "employer", in relation to an employee or a worker, means the person by whom the employee or worker is (or, where the employment has ceased, was) employed.

(5) In this Act "employment"-

(a) in relation to an employee, means employment under a contract of employment; and

(b) in relation to a worker, means employment under his contract;

and "employed" shall be construed accordingly.

55. – (1) In this Act, unless the context otherwise requires,-

> *S.55 - Defines the words and phrases used in the Act*

"civil proceedings" means proceedings before an employment tribunal or civil proceedings before any other court;

"enforcement notice" shall be construed in accordance with section 19 above;

"government department" includes a Northern Ireland department, except in section 52(a) above;

"industrial tribunal" means a tribunal established under Article 3 of the Industrial Tribunals (Northern Ireland) Order 1996;

"notice" means notice in writing;

"pay reference period" shall be construed in accordance with section 1(4) above;

"penalty notice" shall be construed in accordance with section 21 above;

"person who qualifies for the national minimum wage" shall be construed in accordance with section 1(2) above; and related expressions shall be construed accordingly;

"prescribe" means prescribe by regulations;

"regulations" means regulations made by the Secretary of State, except in the case of regulations under section 47(2) or (4) above made by the Secretary of State and the Minister of Agriculture, Fisheries and Food acting jointly or by the Department of Agriculture for Northern Ireland.

(2) Any reference in this Act to a person being remunerated for a pay reference period is a reference to the person being remunerated by his employer in respect of his work in that pay reference period.

(3) Any reference in this Act to doing work includes a reference to performing services; and "work" and other related expressions shall be construed accordingly.

(4) For the purposes of this Act, a person ceases to be of compulsory school age in Scotland when he ceases to be of school age in accordance with sections 31 and 33 of the Education (Scotland) Act 1980.

(5) Any reference in this Act to a person ceasing to be of compulsory school age shall, in relation to Northern Ireland, be construed in accordance with Article 46 of the Education and Libraries (Northern Ireland) Order 1986.

(6) Any reference in this Act to an employment tribunal shall, in relation to Northern Ireland, be construed as a reference to an industrial tribunal.

56. – (1) This Act may be cited as the National Minimum Wage Act 1998.

> *S.56 - Provides the short title for this Act as the National Minimum Wage Act 1998 and for the commencement date to be appointed by the Secretary of State. With effect from 31 July 1998 the Secretary of State is empowered to make orders and Council Regulations or an order. The Act extends to Northern Ireland*

(2) Apart from this section and any powers to make an Order in Council or regulations or an order (which accordingly come into force on the day on which this Act is passed) the provisions of this Act shall come into force on such day or days as the Secretary of State may by order appoint; and different days may be appointed for different purposes.

(3) This Act extends to Northern Ireland.

SCHEDULES

SCHEDULE 1

THE LOW PAY COMMISSION

Membership

1.– (1) The Low Pay Commission appointed under section 8(9) of this Act (in this Schedule referred to as "the Commission") shall consist of a chairman and eight other members appointed by the Secretary of State.

> **Schedule 1**
> *Provides, in respect of the LPC, for its membership, finance, staffing facilities and the regulation of its proceedings. The LPC a specified body in Part II of Schedule 1 to the House of Commons Disqualification Act 1975 and to Part II of Schedule 1 to the Northern Ireland Assembly Disqualification Act 1975. Accordingly specified office holders within the LPC are disqualified from membership of the House of Commons and the Northern Ireland Assembly*

(2) In appointing members, the Secretary of State shall have regard to the desirability of securing that there is such a balance as the Secretary of State considers appropriate between-

    (a) members with knowledge or experience of, or interest in, trade unions or matters relating to workers generally;

    (b) members with knowledge or experience of, or interest in, employers' associations or matters relating to employers generally; and

    (c) members with other relevant knowledge or experience.

(3) Members shall hold and vacate office in accordance with their terms of appointment, subject to the following provisions.

(4) A member may resign his membership by giving notice to the Secretary of State.

(5) A person who ceases to be a member shall be eligible for re-appointment.

(6) The Secretary of State may by notice to the member concerned remove from office a member who-

    (a) has become bankrupt, has made an arrangement with his creditors, has had his estate sequestrated, has granted a trust deed for his creditors or has made a composition contract with his creditors, or

    (b) has been absent from two or more consecutive meetings of the Commission otherwise than for a reason approved by them, or

    (c) is in the opinion of the Secretary of State unable or unfit to perform his duties as member.

Financial provisions

2. – (1) The Secretary of State may pay the members of the Commission such remuneration, and such allowances in respect of travel or other expenses properly incurred by them, or in respect of loss of remuneration sustained by them, in the performance of their duties, as the Secretary of State may determine.

(2) The Secretary of State may determine to pay in respect of a person's office as member of the Commission-

  (a) such pension, allowance or gratuity to or in respect of that person on his retirement or death, or
  (b) such contributions or other payment towards the provision of such a pension, allowance or gratuity,

as the Secretary of State may determine.

(3) Where a person ceases to be a member of the Commission otherwise than on the expiry of his term of office and it appears to the Secretary of State that there are special circumstances which make it right for him to receive compensation, the Secretary of State may determine to make a payment to him by way of compensation of such amount as the Secretary of State may determine.

Staff, facilities and money

3. The Secretary of State shall provide the Commission with-

  (a) such staff,
  (b) such accommodation, equipment and other facilities, and
  (c) such sums,

as the Secretary of State may reasonably determine are required by the Commission for carrying out their duties in preparing any report on matters referred to them under this Act.

Proceedings

4. – (1) The quorum of the Commission and the arrangements relating to their meetings shall be such as the Commission may determine.

(2) The validity of proceedings of the Commission is not affected by-

  (a) any vacancy among the members, whether occurring by reason of death, resignation or otherwise;
  (b) the appointment of a member at any time to fill such a vacancy; or
  (c) any defect in the appointment of a member.

Disqualification for House of Commons and Northern Ireland Assembly

5. – (1) The entry set out in sub-paragraph (2) below shall be inserted at the appropriate place in-

(a) Part II of Schedule 1 to the House of Commons Disqualification Act 1975 (offices disqualifying for membership of the House of Commons); and

(b) Part II of Schedule 1 to the Northern Ireland Assembly Disqualification Act 1975 (offices disqualifying for membership of the Northern Ireland Assembly).

(2) The entry is-

"The Low Pay Commission appointed under section 8(9) of the National Minimum Wage Act 1998."

SCHEDULE 2

AMENDMENTS RELATING TO REMUNERATION ETC OF AGRICULTURAL WORKERS

PART I

THE AGRICULTURAL WAGES ACT 1948

SCHEDULE 2 – Part I

This Part is introduced by s.47 of the Act and extensively amends the Agricultural Wages Act 1948 to provide for its coexistence with the NMW, under the provisions of the Act, whilst preserving the scheme for regulating the remuneration and terms and conditions of employment of agricultural workers in England and Wales

1. The Agricultural Wages Act 1948 shall be amended in accordance with this Part of this Schedule.

Section 3

2. – (1) Section 3 (power of Agricultural Wages Board to fix minimum rates of wages, holiday pay, etc) shall be amended as follows.

(2) After subsection (2A) there shall be inserted-

"(2B) No minimum rate fixed under this section which is an hourly rate shall be less than the national minimum wage.

(2C) No minimum rate fixed under this section which is a rate other than an hourly rate shall be such as to yield a less amount of wages for each hour worked than the hourly amount of the national minimum wage."

(3) After subsection (7) there shall be added-

"(8) If the Board make, or purport to make, an order fixing a minimum rate under this section-

(a) which is an hourly rate but which is lower than the national minimum wage in force when that minimum rate comes into effect, or

(b) which is a rate other than an hourly rate but which is such as to yield a less amount of wages for each hour worked than the hourly amount of the national minimum wage in force when that minimum rate comes into effect,

they shall be taken to have made an order fixing in place of that minimum rate a minimum rate equal to the national minimum wage or, as the case may be, a minimum rate such as to yield an amount of wages for each hour worked equal to the hourly amount of the national minimum wage.

(9) If, at any time after a minimum rate which is an hourly rate comes into effect under this section, the national minimum wage becomes higher than that minimum rate, then, as respects any period beginning at or after that time, the Board shall be taken to have made an order fixing in place of that minimum rate a minimum rate equal to the national minimum wage.

(10)If, at any time after a minimum rate other than an hourly rate comes into effect under this section, the national minimum wage is increased to such a level that that minimum rate yields a less amount of wages for each hour worked than the hourly amount of the national minimum wage, then, as respects any period beginning at or after that time, the Board shall be taken to have made an order fixing in place of that minimum rate a minimum rate such as to yield an amount of wages for each hour worked equal to the hourly amount of the national minimum wage.

(11)Subsections (8) to (10) of this section are without prejudice to the power of the Board to make further orders under this section fixing any minimum rates.

(12)Where an order under this section fixes any particular minimum rate of wages by reference to two or more component rates, of which-

(a) one is the principal component, and

(b) the other or others are supplemental or additional components,

(as in a case where the minimum rate for night work is fixed as the sum of the minimum rate payable in respect of work other than night work and a supplemental or additional minimum rate in respect of working at night) the national minimum wage provisions of this section apply in relation to the principal component rate and not the supplemental or additional component rates.

(13)The national minimum wage provisions of this section do not apply in relation to any minimum rate which is in the nature of an allowance payable in respect of some particular responsibility or circumstance (as in a case where a minimum rate is fixed in respect of being required to keep a dog).

(14)The national minimum wage provisions of this section do not apply in relation to any minimum rate fixed under this section-

(a) by virtue of subsection (2)(d) of this section, or

(b) by virtue of section 67 of the Agriculture Act 1967 (sick pay),

unless and to the extent that regulations under section 2 of the National Minimum Wage Act 1998 make provision which has the effect that circumstances or periods in respect of which the minimum rate in question is required to be paid to a worker are treated as circumstances in which, or times at which, a person is to be regarded as working.

(15) In this section "the national minimum wage provisions of this section" means subsections (2B), (2C) and (8) to (10) of this section."

3. After section 3 there shall be inserted-

"Enforcement.

3A. – (1) The enforcement provisions of the National Minimum Wage Act 1998 shall have effect for the purposes of this Act as they have effect for the purposes of that Act, but with the modifications specified in subsections (3) and (4) of this section.

(2) In subsection (1) of this section "the enforcement provisions of the National Minimum Wage Act 1998" means the following provisions of that Act-

(a) sections 9 to 11 (records);

(b) section 14 (powers of officers);

(c) sections 17 and 19 to 22 (enforcement of right to national minimum wage);

(d) sections 23 and 24 (right not to suffer detriment);

(e) section 28 (evidence: reversal of burden of proof in civil proceedings);

(f) sections 31 to 33 (offences);

(g) section 48 (superior employers); and

(h) section 49 (restriction on contracting out).

(3) In the application of any provision of the National Minimum Wage Act 1998 by subsection (1) of this section-

(a) any reference to that Act, other than a reference to a specific provision of it, includes a reference to this Act;

(b) any reference to a worker (within the meaning of that Act) shall be taken as a reference to a worker employed in agriculture (within the meaning of this Act);

(c) any reference to a person (however described) who qualifies for the national minimum wage shall be taken as a reference to a worker employed in agriculture;

(d) subject to paragraph (c) of this subsection, any reference to the national minimum wage, other than a reference to the hourly amount of the national minimum wage, shall be taken as a reference to the minimum rate applicable under this Act;

(e) subject to paragraph (c) of this subsection, any reference to qualifying for the national minimum wage shall be taken as a reference to being entitled to the minimum rate applicable under this Act;

(f) any reference to a pay reference period shall be disregarded.

(4) In the application of section 33 of the National Minimum Wage Act 1998 (proceedings for offences) by subsection (1) of this section, any reference to the Secretary of State shall be taken to include a reference to the Minister of Agriculture, Fisheries and Food.

(5) In section 104A of the Employment Rights Act 1996 (unfair dismissal: national minimum wage) in subsection (1)(c)-

(a) any reference to a person qualifying for the national minimum wage includes a reference to a person being or becoming entitled to a minimum rate applicable under this Act; and

(b) any reference to a person qualifying for a particular rate of national minimum wage includes a reference to a person being or becoming entitled to a particular minimum rate applicable under this Act."

Section 4

4. – (1) In section 4 (enforcement of wages and holidays orders) the following provisions shall cease to have effect-

(a) in subsection (1)-
   (i) paragraphs (a), (b) and (d) (which relate to wages); and
   (ii) the words from "and, in the case of an offence consisting of a failure to pay wages" onwards;

(b) subsection (2);

(c) in subsection (3), the words "has paid wages at not less than the minimum rate or" and "as the case may be"; and

(d) subsection (4).

(2) In consequence of sub-paragraph (1) above, the sidenote to section 4 becomes "Enforcement of holidays orders".

Section 5

5. – (1) Section 5 (permits to incapacitated persons) shall be amended as follows.

(2) In subsection (1)-

(a) for "the last preceding section relating to payment of wages at not less than the minimum rate" there shall be substituted "subsection (1) of section 31 of the National Minimum Wage Act 1998 as it applies for the purposes of this Act (offence of refusing or wilfully neglecting to pay worker at applicable rate)"; and

(b) for "any legal proceedings under the last preceding section for failing" there shall be substituted "any legal proceedings under that subsection, as it so applies, for refusing or wilfully neglecting".

(3) After subsection (1) there shall be inserted-

"(1A) Every permit under subsection (1) of this section (whenever granted) shall be deemed to contain a condition that the worker to whom it is granted must at any time be paid at a rate which-

(a) in the case of an hourly rate, is not less than the national minimum wage in force at that time; or
(b) in the case of a rate other than an hourly rate, is such as to yield an amount of wages for each hour worked which is not less than the hourly amount of the national minimum wage in force at that time.

(1B) The condition which a permit is deemed to contain by virtue of subsection (1A) of this section-

(a) overrides any other condition which the permit contains as to payment of wages, to the extent that that other condition provides for payment of wages at any time at a lower rate; but
(b) is without prejudice to any other condition which the permit contains as to payment of wages, to the extent that that other condition provides for payment of wages at any time at a higher rate."

(4) In subsection (2)-

(a) for "the preceding subsection" there shall be substituted "subsection (1) of this section"; and
(b) for "any legal proceedings under the last preceding section for failing" there shall be substituted "any legal proceedings under section 31(1) of the National Minimum Wage Act 1998, as it applies for the purposes of this Act, for refusing or wilfully neglecting".

Section 11

6. Section 11(1)(a) (invalidity of certain agreements) shall cease to have effect.

Section 12

7. – (1) Section 12 (officers) shall be amended as follows.

(2) In subsection (5)(a) (power to institute civil proceedings on behalf of worker on account of payment of wages at less than the applicable minimum rate etc) the words "on account of the payment of wages to him at less than the minimum rate applicable or" shall cease to have effect.

(3) At the end of the section there shall be added-

"(8) The powers conferred by subsections (3) and (4) of this section are not exercisable in any case where corresponding or similar powers conferred by any of the enforcement provisions of the National Minimum Wage Act 1998, as they have effect for the purposes of this Act, are exercisable by virtue of section 3A of this Act.

(9) In subsection (8) of this section, "the enforcement provisions of the National Minimum Wage Act 1998" has the same meaning as in subsection (1) of section 3A of this Act."

Information obtained by national minimum wage officers

8. After section 15 there shall be inserted-

"15A. – (1) This section applies to information which has been obtained by an officer acting for the purposes of the National Minimum Wage Act 1998.

(2) This section does not apply to any information to the extent that the information relates to-

(a) any failure to allow holidays directed to be allowed by an order under section 3 of this Act; or
(b) any terms and conditions of employment fixed by such an order by virtue of subsection (1)(c) of that section.

(3) Information to which this section applies may, with the authority of the Secretary of State, be supplied to the relevant Minister for use for any purpose relating to this Act.

(4) Information supplied under subsection (3) of this section shall not be supplied by the recipient to any other person or body unless-

(a) it could be supplied to that person or body under that subsection; or
(b) it is supplied for the purposes of any civil or criminal proceedings relating to this Act;

and shall not be supplied in those circumstances without the authority of the Secretary of State.

(5) This section does not limit the circumstances in which information may be supplied or used apart from this section.

(6) In this section "the relevant Minister" means-

(a) in relation to England, the Minister of Agriculture, Fisheries and Food; and
(b) in relation to Wales, the Minister of the Crown with the function of appointing officers under section 12 of this Act in relation to Wales."

Section 17

9. – (1) Section 17 (interpretation) shall be amended as follows.

(2) In subsection (1) the following definition shall be inserted at the appropriate place-

" "the national minimum wage" means the single hourly rate for the time being in force by virtue of regulations under section 1(3) of the National Minimum Wage Act 1998, but this definition is subject to subsection (1A) of this section;".

(3) After subsection (1) there shall be inserted-

"(1A) If, in the case of persons of any description, regulations under subsection (2) of section 3 of the National Minimum Wage Act 1998-

(a) prevent them being persons who (within the meaning of that Act) qualify for the national minimum wage, or

(b) prescribe a rate ("the reduced rate") for the national minimum wage other than the single hourly rate for the time being prescribed under section 1(3) of that Act,

this Act shall have effect in relation to persons of that description as if in a case falling within paragraph (a) above the national minimum wage were nil and in a case falling within paragraph (b) above the national minimum wage were the reduced rate."

Relationship between the national minimum wage and agricultural wages legislation

10. After section 17 there shall be inserted-

"17A. – (1) Except so far as expressly provided by this Act, nothing in the National Minimum Wage Act 1998 or in regulations made under that Act affects the operation of this Act.

(2) This Act is subject to-

(a) section 46 of the National Minimum Wage Act 1998; and

(b) section 47 of that Act and any regulations made under that section."

PART II

THE AGRICULTURAL WAGES (SCOTLAND) ACT 1949

SCHEDULE 2 – Part II
This Part is introduced by s.47 of the Act and extensively amends the Agricultural Wages Act 1948 to provide for its coexistence with the NMW, under the provisions of the Act, whilst preserving the scheme for regulating the remuneration and terms and conditions of employment of agricultural workers in Scotland

11. The Agricultural Wages (Scotland) Act 1949 shall be amended in accordance with this Part of this Schedule.

Section 3

12. – (1) Section 3 (power of Scottish Agricultural Wages Board to fix minimum rates of wages, holidays to be allowed etc.) shall be amended as follows.

(2) After subsection (2A) there shall be inserted-

"(2B) No minimum rate fixed under this section which is an hourly rate shall be less than the national minimum wage.

(2C) No minimum rate fixed under this section which is a rate other than an hourly rate shall be such as to yield a less amount of wages for each hour worked than the hourly amount of the national minimum wage."

(3) After subsection (7) there shall be added-

"(8) If the Board makes, or purports to make, an order fixing a minimum rate under this section-

(a) which is an hourly rate but which is lower than the national minimum wage in force when that minimum rate comes into effect, or
(b) which is a rate other than an hourly rate but which is such as to yield a less amount of wages for each hour worked than the hourly amount of the national minimum wage in force when that minimum rate comes into effect,

the Board shall be taken to have made an order fixing in place of that minimum rate a minimum rate equal to the national minimum wage or, as the case may be, a minimum rate such as to yield an amount of wages for each hour worked equal to the hourly amount of the national minimum wage.

(9) If, at any time after a minimum rate which is an hourly rate comes into effect under this section, the national minimum wage becomes higher than that minimum rate, then, as respects any period beginning at or after that time, the Board shall be taken to have made an order fixing in place of that minimum rate a minimum rate equal to the national minimum wage.

(10)If, at any time after a minimum rate other than an hourly rate comes into effect under this section, the national minimum wage is increased to such a level that that minimum rate yields a less amount of wages for each hour worked than the hourly amount of the national minimum wage, then, as respects any period beginning at or after that time, the Board shall be taken to have made an order fixing in place of that minimum rate a minimum rate such as to yield an amount of wages for each hour worked equal to the hourly amount of the national minimum wage.

(11) Subsections (8) to (10) of this section are without prejudice to the power of the Board to make further orders under this section fixing any minimum rates.

(12) Where an order under this section fixes any particular minimum rate of wages by reference to two or more component rates, of which-

(a) one is the principal component, and

(b) the other or others are supplemental or additional components,

(as in a case where the minimum rate for night work is fixed as the sum of the minimum rate payable in respect of work other than night work and a supplemental or additional minimum rate in respect of working at night) the national minimum wage provisions of this section apply in relation to the principal component rate and not the supplemental or additional component rates.

(13) The national minimum wage provisions of this section do not apply in relation to any minimum rate which is in the nature of an allowance payable in respect of some particular responsibility or circumstance (as in a case where a minimum rate is fixed in respect of being required to keep a dog).

(14) The national minimum wage provisions of this section do not apply in relation to any minimum rate fixed under this section-

(a) by virtue of subsection (2)(d) of this section, or

(b) by virtue of section 67 of the Agriculture Act 1967 (sick pay),

unless and to the extent that regulations under section 2 of the National Minimum Wage Act 1998 make provision which has the effect that circumstances or periods in respect of which the minimum rate in question is required to be paid to a worker are treated as circumstances in which, or times at which, a person is to be regarded as working.

(15) In this section "the national minimum wage provisions of this section" means subsections (2B), (2C) and (8) to (10) of this section."

Enforcement

13. After section 3 there shall be inserted-

"3A. – (1) The enforcement provisions of the National Minimum Wage Act 1998 shall have effect for the purposes of this Act as they have effect for the purposes of that Act, but with the modifications specified in subsection (3) of this section.

(2) In subsection (1) of this section "the enforcement provisions of the National Minimum Wage Act 1998" means the following provisions of that Act-

(a) sections 9 to 11 (records);

(b) section 14 (powers of officers);

(c) sections 17 and 19 to 22 (enforcement of right to national minimum wage);

(d) sections 23 and 24 (right not to suffer detriment);

(e) section 28 (evidence: reversal of burden of proof in civil proceedings);

(f) sections 31, 32 and 33(4) and (5) (offences);

(g) section 48 (superior employees); and

(h) section 49 (restriction on contracting out).

(3) In the application of any provision of the National Minimum Wage Act 1998 by subsection (1) of this section-

(a) any reference to that Act, other than a reference to a specific provision of it, includes a reference to this Act;

(b) any reference to a worker (within the meaning of that Act) shall be taken as a reference to a worker employed in agriculture (within the meaning of this Act);

(c) any reference to a person (however described) who qualifies for the national minimum wage shall be taken as a reference to a worker employed in agriculture;

(d) subject to paragraph (c) of this subsection, any reference to the national minimum wage, other than a reference to the hourly amount of the national minimum wage, shall be taken as a reference to the minimum rate applicable under this Act;

(e) subject to paragraph (c) of this subsection, any reference to qualifying for the national minimum wage shall be taken as a reference to being entitled to the minimum rate applicable under this Act; and

(f) any reference to a pay reference period shall be disregarded.

(4) In section 104A of the Employment Rights Act 1996 (unfair dismissal: national minimum wage) in subsection (1)(c)-

(a) any reference to a person qualifying for the national minimum wage includes a reference to a person being or becoming entitled to a minimum rate applicable under this Act; and

(b) any reference to a person qualifying for a particular rate of national minimum wage includes a reference to a person being or becoming entitled to a particular minimum rate applicable under this Act."

Section 4

14. In section 4 (enforcement of wages and holiday orders) the following provisions shall cease to have effect-

(a) in subsection (1)-
   (i) paragraphs (a), (b) and (d); and
   (ii) the words "and, in the case of an offence consisting of a failure to pay wages" onwards;

(b) subsection (2);

(c) in subsection (3), the words "has paid wages at not less than the minimum rate of" and ", as the case may be"; and

(d) subsection (4).

Section 5

15. – (1) Section 5 (permits to infirm and incapacitated persons) shall be amended as follows.

(2) In subsection (1)-

(a) for "the last preceding section relating to payment of wages at not less than the minimum rate" there shall be substituted "subsection (1) of section 31 of the National Minimum Wage Act 1998 as it applies for the purposes of this Act (offence of refusing or wilfully neglecting to pay worker at applicable rate)"; and

(b) for "any legal proceedings under the last preceding section for failing" there shall be substituted "any legal proceedings under that subsection, as it so applies, for refusing or wilfully neglecting".

(3) After subsection (1) there shall be inserted-

"(1A) Every permit under subsection (1) of this section (whenever granted) shall be deemed to contain a condition that the worker to whom it is granted must at any time be paid at a rate which-

(a) in the case of an hourly rate, is not less than the national minimum wage in force at that time, or

(b) in the case of a rate other than an hourly rate, is such as to yield an amount of wages for each hour worked which is not less than the hourly amount of the national minimum wage in force at that time.

(1B)   The condition which a permit is deemed to contain by virtue of subsection (1A) of this section-

(a) overrides any other condition which the permit contains as to payment of wages, to the extent that that other condition provides for payment of wages at any time at a lower rate; but

(b) is without prejudice to any other condition which the permit contains as to payment of wages, to the extent that that other condition provides for payment of wages at any time at a higher rate."

(4) In subsection (2)-

(a) for "the preceding subsection" there shall be substituted "subsection (1) of this section"; and

(b) for "any legal proceedings under the last preceding section for failing" there shall be substituted "any legal proceedings under section 31(1) of the National Minimum Wage Act 1998, as it applies for the purposes of this Act, for refusing or wilfully neglecting".

Section 11

16. Section 11(1)(a) (invalidity of certain agreements) shall cease to have effect.

Section 12

17. – (1) Section 12 (officers) shall be amended as follows.

(2) Subsection (4)(a) (power to institute civil proceedings on behalf of worker on account of payment of wages at less than the applicable minimum rate etc) shall cease to have effect.

(3) At the end of the section there shall be added-

"(7) The powers conferred by subsection (3) of this section are not exercisable in any case where corresponding or similar powers conferred by any of the enforcement provisions of the National Minimum Wage Act 1998, as they have effect for the purposes of this Act, are exercisable by virtue of section 3A of this Act.

(8) In subsection (7) of this section, "the enforcement provisions of the National Minimum Wage Act 1998" has the same meaning as in subsection (1) of section 3A of this Act."

Information obtained by national minimum wage officers

18. After section 15 there shall be inserted-

"15A. – (1) This section applies to information which has been obtained by an officer acting for the purposes of the National Minimum Wage Act 1998.

(2) This section does not apply to any information to the extent that the information relates to-

(a) any failure to allow holidays directed to be allowed by an order under section 3 of this Act; or

(b) any terms and conditions of employment fixed by such an order by virtue of subsection (1)(c) of that section.

(3) Information to which this section applies may, with the authority of the relevant Minister, be supplied to the Secretary of State for use for any purpose relating to this Act.

(4) Information supplied under subsection (3) of this section shall not be supplied by the recipient to any other person or body unless-

(a) it could be supplied to that person or body under that subsection; or

(b) it is supplied for the purposes of any civil or criminal proceedings relating to this Act;

and shall not be supplied in those circumstances without the authority of the relevant Minister.

(5) This section does not limit the circumstances in which information may be supplied or used apart from this section.

(6) In this section "the relevant Minister" means the Minister of the Crown with the function of appointing officers under section 13(1)(a) of the National Minimum Wage Act 1998."

Section 17

19. – (1) Section 17 (interpretation) shall be amended as follows.

(2) In subsection (1) the following definition shall be inserted in the appropriate place-

" "the national minimum wage" means the single hourly rate for the time being in force by virtue of regulations under section 1(3) of the National Minimum Wage Act 1998, but this definition is subject to subsection (1A) of this section;".

(3) After subsection (1) there shall be inserted-

"(1A) If, in the case of persons of any description, regulations under subsection (2) of section 3 of the National Minimum Wage Act 1998-

(a) prevent them being persons who (within the meaning of that Act) qualify for the national minimum wage; or
(b) prescribe a rate ("the reduced rate") for the national minimum wage other than the single hourly rate for the time being prescribed under section 1(3) of that Act,

this Act shall have effect in relation to persons of that description as if in a case falling within paragraph (a) above the national minimum wage were nil and in a case falling within paragraph (b) above the national minimum wage were the reduced rate."

Relationship between national minimum wage and agricultural wages legislation

20. After section 17 there shall be inserted-

"17A. – (1) Except so far as expressly provided by this Act, nothing in the National Minimum Wage Act 1998 or in regulations made under that Act affects the operation of this Act.

(2) This Act is subject to-

(a) section 46 of the National Minimum Wage Act 1998; and
(b) section 47 of that Act and any regulations made under that section."

PART III

THE AGRICULTURAL WAGES (REGULATION) (NORTHERN IRELAND) ORDER 1977

SCHEDULE 2 – Part III
This Part is introduced by s.47 of the Act and extensively amends the Agricultural Wages Act 1948 to provide for its coexistence with the NMW, under the provisions of the Act, whilst preserving the scheme for regulating the remuneration and terms and conditions of employment of agricultural workers in Northern Ireland

21. The Agricultural Wages (Regulation) (Northern Ireland) Order 1977 shall be amended in accordance with this Part of this Schedule.

Article 2

22. – (1) Article 2 (interpretation) shall be amended as follows.

(2) In paragraph (2) the following definition shall be inserted at the appropriate place-

" "the national minimum wage" means the single hourly rate for the time being in force by virtue of regulations under section 1(3) of the National Minimum Wage Act 1998, but this definition is subject to paragraph (2A);".

(3) After paragraph (2) there shall be inserted-

"(2A) If, in the case of persons of any description, regulations under subsection (2) of section 3 of the National Minimum Wage Act 1998-

(a) prevent them being persons who (within the meaning of that Act) qualify for the national minimum wage, or

(b) prescribe a rate ("the reduced rate") for the national minimum wage other than the single hourly rate for the time being prescribed under section 1(3) of that Act,

this Order shall have effect in relation to persons of that description as if in a case falling within sub-paragraph (a) the national minimum wage were nil and in a case falling within sub-paragraph (b) the national minimum wage were the reduced rate."

Relationship between the national minimum wage and agricultural wages legislation

23. After Article 2 there shall be inserted-

"Relationship between this Order and the National Minimum Wage Act 1998.

2A. – (1) Except so far as expressly provided by this Order, nothing in the National

Minimum Wage Act 1998 or in regulations made under that Act affects the operation of this Order.

(2) This Order is subject to-

(a) section 46 of the National Minimum Wage Act 1998; and

(b) section 47 of that Act and any regulations made under that section."

Article 4

24. – (1) Article 4 (power of Agricultural Wages Board for Northern Ireland to fix minimum rates of wages) shall be amended as follows.

(2) After paragraph (1) there shall be inserted-

"(1A) No minimum rate fixed under this Article which is an hourly rate shall be less than the national minimum wage.

(1B)   No minimum rate fixed under this Article which is a rate other than an hourly rate shall be such as to yield a less amount of wages for each hour worked than the hourly amount of the national minimum wage."

(3) After paragraph (12) there shall be added-

"(13) If the Board makes, or purports to make, an order fixing a minimum rate under this Article-

(a) which is an hourly rate but which is lower than the national minimum wage in force when that minimum rate comes into effect, or

(b) which is a rate other than an hourly rate but which is such as to yield a less amount of wages for each hour worked than the hourly amount of the national minimum wage in force when that minimum rate comes into effect,

the Board shall be taken to have made an order fixing in place of that minimum rate a minimum rate equal to the national minimum wage or, as the case may be, a minimum rate such as to yield an amount of wages for each hour worked equal to the hourly amount of the national minimum wage.

(14) If, at any time after a minimum rate which is an hourly rate comes into effect under this Article, the national minimum wage becomes higher than that minimum rate, then, as respects any period beginning at or after that time, the Board shall be taken to have made an order fixing in place of that minimum rate a minimum rate equal to the national minimum wage.

(15) If, at any time after a minimum rate other than an hourly rate comes into effect under this Article, the national minimum wage is increased to such a level that that minimum rate yields a less amount of wages for each hour worked than the hourly amount of the national minimum wage, then, as respects any period beginning at or after that time, the Board shall be taken to have made an order fixing in place of that minimum rate a minimum rate such as to yield an

amount of wages for each hour worked equal to the hourly amount of the national minimum wage.

(16) Paragraphs (13) to (15) are without prejudice to the power of the Board to make further orders under this Article fixing any minimum rates.

(17) Where an order under this Article fixes any particular minimum rate of wages by reference to two or more component rates, of which-

(a) one is the principal component, and

(b) the other or others are supplemental or additional components,

(as in a case where the minimum rate for night work is fixed as the sum of the minimum rate payable in respect of work other than night work and a supplemental or additional minimum rate in respect of working at night) the national minimum wage provisions of this Article apply in relation to the principal component rate and not the supplemental or additional component rates.

(18) The national minimum wage provisions of this Article do not apply in relation to any minimum rate which is in the nature of an allowance payable in respect of some particular responsibility or circumstance (as in a case where a minimum rate is fixed in respect of being required to keep a dog).

(19) The national minimum wage provisions of this Article do not apply in relation to any minimum rate fixed under this Article by virtue of Article 5 or 8(5), unless and to the extent that regulations under section 2 of the National Minimum Wage Act 1998 make provision which has the effect that circumstances or periods in respect of which the minimum rate in question is required to be paid to a worker employed in agriculture are treated as circumstances in which, or times at which, a person is to be regarded as working.

(20) In this Article "the national minimum wage provisions of this Article" means paragraphs (1A), (1B) and (13) to (15)."

Article 6

25. – (1) Article 6 (permits exempting, in certain cases, payment of minimum rate) shall be amended as follows.

(2) In paragraph (1), after "the employment of the worker from" there shall be inserted "(a)" and after "not less than the minimum rate" there shall be inserted the word "or" and the following sub-paragraph-

"(b) any legal proceedings under section 31(1) of the National Minimum Wage Act 1998 as it applies for the purposes of this Order (offence of refusing or wilfully neglecting to pay worker at applicable rate),".

(3) After paragraph (1) there shall be inserted-

"(1A) Every permit under paragraph (1) (whenever granted) shall be deemed to contain a condition that the worker to whom it is granted must at any time be paid at a rate which-

(a) in the case of an hourly rate, is not less than the national minimum wage in force at that time, or

(b) in the case of a rate other than an hourly rate, is such as to yield an amount of wages for each hour worked which is not less than the hourly amount of the national minimum wage in force at that time.

(1B) The condition which a permit is deemed to contain by virtue of paragraph (1A)-

(a) overrides any other condition which the permit contains as to payment of wages, to the extent that that other condition provides for payment of wages at any time at a lower rate; but

(b) is without prejudice to any other condition which the permit contains as to payment of wages, to the extent that that other condition provides for payment of wages at any time at a higher rate."

(4) In paragraph (2), after "shall not be liable to" there shall be inserted "(a)" and after "less than the minimum rate," there shall be inserted the word "or" and the following sub-paragraph-

"(b) any legal proceedings under section 31(1) of the National Minimum Wage Act 1998 as it applies for the purposes of this Order,".

(5) In paragraph (3), after "any legal proceedings" there shall be inserted "(a)" and after "under this Order" there shall be inserted the word "or" and the following sub-paragraph-

"(b) under section 31(1) of the National Minimum Wage Act 1998 as it applies for the purposes of this Order,".

Enforcement

26. After Article 8 there shall be inserted-

"Enforcement.

8A. – (1) The enforcement provisions of the National Minimum Wage Act 1998 shall have effect for the purposes of this Order as they have effect for the purposes of that Act, but with the modifications specified in paragraphs (3) and (4).

(2) In paragraph (1) "the enforcement provisions of the National Minimum Wage Act 1998" means the following provisions of that Act-

(a) sections 9 to 11 (records);

(b) section 14 (powers of officers);

(c) sections 17 and 19 to 22 (enforcement of right to national minimum wage);

(d) sections 23 and 24 (right not to suffer detriment);

(e) section 28 (evidence: reversal of burden of proof in civil proceedings);

(f) sections 31 to 33 (offences);

(g) section 48 (superior employers); and

(h) section 49 (restriction on contracting out).

(3) In the application of any provision of the National Minimum Wage Act 1998 by paragraph (1)-

(a) any reference to that Act, other than a reference to a specific provision of it, includes a reference to this Order;

(b) any reference to a worker (within the meaning of that Act) shall be taken as a reference to a worker employed in agriculture (within the meaning of this Order);

(c) any reference to a person (however described) who qualifies for the national minimum wage shall be taken as a reference to a worker employed in agriculture;

(d) subject to sub-paragraph (c), any reference to the national minimum wage, other than a reference to the hourly amount of the national minimum wage, shall be taken as a reference to the minimum rate applicable under this Order;

(e) subject to sub-paragraph (c), any reference to qualifying for the national minimum wage shall be taken as a reference to being entitled to the minimum rate applicable under this Order; and

(f) any reference to a pay reference period shall be disregarded.

(4) In the application of section 33 of the National Minimum Wage Act 1998 (proceedings for offences) by paragraph (1), any reference to the Secretary of State shall be taken to include a reference to the Department of Agriculture for Northern Ireland.

(5) In Article 135A of the Employment Rights (Northern Ireland) Order 1996 (unfair dismissal: national minimum wage) in paragraph (1)(c)-

(a) any reference to a person qualifying for the national minimum wage includes a reference to a person being or becoming entitled to a minimum rate applicable under this Order; and

(b) any reference to a person qualifying for a particular rate of national minimum wage includes a reference to a person being or becoming entitled to a particular minimum rate applicable under this Order."

Information obtained by national minimum wage officers

27. After Article 11 there shall be inserted-

"Information obtained by national minimum wage officers.

11A. – (1) This Article applies to information which has been obtained by an officer acting for the purposes of the National Minimum Wage Act 1998.

(2) This Article does not apply to any information to the extent that the information relates to any failure to allow holidays in accordance with Article 8.

(3) Information to which this Article applies may, with the authority of the Secretary of State, be supplied to the Department for use for any purpose relating to this Order.

(4) Information supplied under paragraph (3) shall not be supplied by the recipient to any other person or body unless-

(a) it could be supplied to that person or body under that paragraph; or
(b) it is supplied for the purposes of any civil or criminal proceedings relating to this Order;

and shall not be supplied in those circumstances without the authority of the Secretary of State.

(5) This Article does not limit the circumstances in which information may be supplied or used apart from this Article."

SCHEDULE 3

REPEALS AND REVOCATIONS

SCHEDULE 3
A table of consequential repeals and revocations

Chapter	Short title	Extent of repeal or revocation
11 & 12 Geo. 6c. 47.	The Agricultural Wages Act 1948.	In section 4, in subsection (1), paragraphs (a), (b) and (d) and the words from "and, in the case of an offence consisting of a failure to pay wages" onwards, subsection (2), in subsection (3), the words "has paid wages at not less than the minimum rate or" and "as the case may be", and subsection (4). Section 7(2). Section 11(1)(a).

Chapter	Short title	Extent of repeal or revocation
11 & 12 Geo. 6c. 47.–*contd.*		In section 12(5)(a), the words "on account of the payment of wages to him at less than the minimum rate applicable or".
12 & 13 Geo. 6 c. 30.	The Agricultural Wages (Scotland) Act 1949.	In section 4, in subsection (1), paragraphs (a), (b) and (d) and the words "and, in the case of an offence consisting of a failure to pay wages" onwards, subsection (2), in subsection (3), the words "has paid wages at not less than the minimum rate of" and ", as the case may be" and subsection (4).
		Section 11(1)(a).
		Section 12(4)(a).
1996 c. 17.	The Employment Tribunals Act 1996.	In section 21(1)(f), the word "or".
1996 c. 18.	The Employment Rights Act 1996.	In section 108(3), the word "or" at the end of paragraph (g).
		In section 109(2), the word "or" at the end of paragraph (g).
S.I. 1996/1919 (N.I.16).	The Employment Rights (Northern Ireland) Order 1996.	In Article 142(2), the word "or" at the end of sub-paragraph (b).

Public Interest Disclosure Act 1998

1998 c. 23

An Act to protect individuals who make certain disclosures of information in the public interest; to allow such individuals to bring action in respect of victimisation; and for connected purposes.

[2nd July 1998]

> *All provisions of the Act have been in force since 2 July 1999*

Be it enacted by the Queen's most Excellent Majesty, by and with the advice and consent of the Lords Spiritual and Temporal, and Commons, in this present Parliament assembled, and by the authority of the same, as follows:-

1. After Part IV of the Employment Rights Act 1996 (in this Act referred to as "the 1996 Act") there is inserted-

> *S.1   This Act adds Part IVA (consisting of s.43A-43L) to the Employment Rights Act 1996 between Part IV (Sunday Working for Shop and Betting Workers) and Part V (Protection from Suffering Detriment in Employment)*

"PART IVA

PROTECTED DISCLOSURES

43A.   In this Act a "protected disclosure" means a qualifying disclosure (as defined by section 43B) which is made by a worker in accordance with any of sections 43C to 43H.

> *In order for a public disclosure by a worker to attract the protection of the Act, the disclosure in question must fall into one of the specified categories of subject matter set out in s.43B below AND the disclosure must be made in one of the specified manners of procedure set out in s.43C-43H below*

43B. – (1) In this Part a "qualifying disclosure" means any disclosure of information which, in the reasonable belief of the worker making the disclosure, tends to show one or more of the following-

(a) that a criminal offence has been committed, is being committed or is likely to be committed,

(b) that a person has failed, is failing or is likely to fail to comply with any legal obligation to which he is subject,

(c) that a miscarriage of justice has occurred, is occurring or is likely to occur,

(d) that the health or safety of any individual has been, is being or is likely to be endangered,

(e) that the environment has been, is being or is likely to be damaged, or

(f) that information tending to show any matter falling within any one of the preceding paragraphs has been, is being or is likely to be deliberately concealed.

The six categories of subject matter relate to:

- *The commission of a criminal offence*

- *Non-compliance with any legal obligation*

- *A miscarriage of justice*

- *Health and safety dangers*

  Damage to the environment

- *The deliberate concealment of such matters – "the relevant failure"*

(2) For the purposes of subsection (1), it is immaterial whether the relevant failure occurred, occurs or would occur in the United Kingdom or elsewhere, and whether the law applying to it is that of the United Kingdom or of any other country or territory.

Protected disclosures can relate to relevant failures occurring anywhere in the world

(3) A disclosure of information is not a qualifying disclosure if the person making the disclosure commits an offence by making it.

A protected disclosure loses its protection if the person making the disclosure commits an offence by making it.

Arguably the Employment Tribunal should adopt the criminal standard of proof when determining the question of whether the employee is unprotected under this provision i.e. whether the totality of the evidence satisfies the Employment Tribunal beyond reasonable doubt that the Applicant has committed an offence by making the disclosure, rather than determining the matter on the conventional basis of the balance of probabilities

(4) A disclosure of information in respect of which a claim to legal professional privilege (or, in Scotland, to confidentiality as between client and professional legal adviser) could be maintained in legal proceedings is not a qualifying disclosure if it is made by a person to whom the information had been disclosed in the course of obtaining legal advice.

The effect of this section is that if the legal adviser, because of the rules regarding legal professional privilege, cannot be compelled to give evidence in Court regarding an issue, the legal adviser cannot make a protected disclosure. The combined effect with s.43D is that a worker can seek legal advice on an area of concern and be protected

(5) In this Part "the relevant failure", in relation to a qualifying disclosure, means the matter falling within paragraphs (a) to (f) of subsection (1).

The phrase "the relevant failure" means the relevant subject matter of the protected disclosure under s.43B(1)

43C. – (1) A qualifying disclosure is made in accordance with this section if the worker makes the disclosure in good faith-

Protection is dependent on compliance with the specified procedures which must be followed when disclosing the relevant failure. The first of these is a disclosure in good faith made to the worker's employer or alternatively where the worker reasonably believes the relevant failure relates solely or mainly to the conduct of a third party, or any other matter for which the third party has legal responsibility, to that third party

(a) to his employer, or

(b) where the worker reasonably believes that the relevant failure relates solely or mainly to-

(i) the conduct of a person other than his employer, or

(ii) any other matter for which a person other than his employer has legal responsibility,

to that other person.

(2) A worker who, in accordance with a procedure whose use by him is authorised by his employer, makes a qualifying disclosure to a person other than his employer, is to be treated for the purposes of this Part as making the qualifying disclosure to his employer.

Disclosure by a worker to a third party is treated as a disclosure to the worker's employer where the disclosure is in accordance with a procedure authorised by the employer

43D. A qualifying disclosure is made in accordance with this section if it is made in the course of obtaining legal advice.

This provision should be read in conjunction with s.43B(4). This is the only protected disclosure which does not have to be made in good faith

43E. A qualifying disclosure is made in accordance with this section if-

(a) the worker's employer is-

(i) an individual appointed under any enactment by a Minister of the Crown, or

(ii) a body any of whose members are so appointed, and

(b) the disclosure is made in good faith to a Minister of the Crown.

A disclosure has statutory protection where it is made in good faith to a Minister of the Crown and the worker's employer is either an individual appointed under any enactment by a Minister of the Crown, or a body, any of whose members are so appointed

43F. – (1) A qualifying disclosure is made in accordance with this section if the worker-

(a) makes the disclosure in good faith to a person prescribed by an order made by the Secretary of State for the purposes of this section, and
(b) reasonably believes-
   (i) that the relevant failure falls within any description of matters in respect of which that person is so prescribed, and
   (ii) that the information disclosed, and any allegation contained in it, are substantially true.

(2) An order prescribing persons for the purposes of this section may specify persons or descriptions of persons, and shall specify the descriptions of matters in respect of which each person, or persons of each description, is or are prescribed.

Disclosure will be protected if it is made in good faith to a person prescribed by an Order made by the Secretary of State and the worker reasonably believes that the disclosure is protected as a relevant failure under the Act and that the material disclosed is substantially true. The Public Interest Disclosure (Prescribed Persons) Order 1999 - SI.1999/1549 came into force on 2 July 1999

43G. – (1) A qualifying disclosure is made in accordance with this section if-

(a) the worker makes the disclosure in good faith,
(b) he reasonably believes that the information disclosed, and any allegation contained in it, are substantially true,
(c) he does not make the disclosure for purposes of personal gain,
(d) any of the conditions in subsection (2) is met, and
(e) in all the circumstances of the case, it is reasonable for him to make the disclosure.

(2) The conditions referred to in subsection (1)(d) are-

(a) that, at the time he makes the disclosure, the worker reasonably believes that he will be subjected to a detriment by his employer if he makes a disclosure to his employer or in accordance with section 43F,

(b) that, in a case where no person is prescribed for the purposes of section 43F in relation to the relevant failure, the worker reasonably believes that it is likely that evidence relating to the relevant failure will be concealed or destroyed if he makes a disclosure to his employer, or

(c) that the worker has previously made a disclosure of substantially the same information-

    (i) to his employer, or

    (ii) in accordance with section 43F.

(3) In determining for the purposes of subsection (1)(e) whether it is reasonable for the worker to make the disclosure, regard shall be had, in particular, to-

(a) the identity of the person to whom the disclosure is made,

(b) the seriousness of the relevant failure,

(c) whether the relevant failure is continuing or is likely to occur in the future,

(d) whether the disclosure is made in breach of a duty of confidentiality owed by the employer to any other person,

(e) in a case falling within subsection (2)(c)(i) or (ii), any action which the employer or the person to whom the previous disclosure in accordance with section 43F was made has taken or might reasonably be expected to have taken as a result of the previous disclosure, and

(f) in a case falling within subsection (2)(c)(i), whether in making the disclosure to the employer the worker complied with any procedure whose use by him was authorised by the employer.

(4) For the purposes of this section a subsequent disclosure may be regarded as a disclosure of substantially the same information as that disclosed by a previous disclosure as mentioned in subsection (2)(c) even though the subsequent disclosure extends to information about action taken or not taken by any person as a result of the previous disclosure.

S.43G of the Employment Rights Act 1996 provides a general broad category of protected disclosures. The protection applies if the worker makes a disclosure in good faith; reasonably believing that the information disclosed and any allegations contained in it, are substantially true; does not make the disclosure for the purposes of personal gain; satisfies one of the following conditions; and in all the circumstances of the case, it is reasonable to make the disclosure

The qualifying conditions are that at the time of making the disclosure the worker reasonably believes that he will be subjected to a detriment by his employer if he makes a disclosure to his employer or to a person in the Prescribed Persons Order 1999 or where there is no prescribed person, the worker reasonably believes that it is likely that evidence will be concealed or destroyed if he makes a disclosure to his employer; or the worker has previously made a disclosure of substantially the same information to his employer or to a prescribed person. In determining the reasonableness of the disclosure the Employment Tribunal will pay particular but not exclusive regard to the identity of the person to whom disclosure is made, the seriousness of the relevant failure; whether the relevant failure is continuing or is likely to occur in the future; whether the disclosure is in breach of a duty of confidentiality owed by the employer to any other person; in a case where the worker has previously made a disclosure of substantially the same information to his employer or a prescribed person, any action which such person has taken, or might reasonably be expected to take, as a result of the previous disclosure and where the worker has previously made a disclosure of substantially the same information to his previous employer whether the worker has complied with any procedure authorised by the employer

43H. – (1) A qualifying disclosure is made in accordance with this section if-

    (a) the worker makes the disclosure in good faith,

    (b) he reasonably believes that the information disclosed, and any allegation contained in it, are substantially true,

    (c) he does not make the disclosure for purposes of personal gain,

    (d) the relevant failure is of an exceptionally serious nature, and

    (e) in all the circumstances of the case, it is reasonable for him to make the disclosure.

(2) In determining for the purposes of subsection (1)(e) whether it is reasonable for the worker to make the disclosure, regard shall be had, in particular, to the identity of the person to whom the disclosure is made.

It is a qualifying disclosure if the worker makes the disclosure in good faith; he reasonably believes the information disclosed and any allegation contained in it are substantially true; he does not make the disclosure for the purposes of personal gain; the relevant failure is of an exceptionally serious nature; and in all the circumstances of the case it is reasonable for him to make the disclosure. The Employment Tribunal is directed, in connection with the reasonableness of the disclosure, to have regard in particular but not exclusively to the identity of the person to whom the disclosure is made

43J. – (1) Any provision in an agreement to which this section applies is void in so far as it purports to preclude the worker from making a protected disclosure.

(2) This section applies to any agreement between a worker and his employer (whether a worker's contract or not), including an agreement to refrain from instituting or continuing any proceedings under this Act or any proceedings for breach of contract.

Any provision in an agreement between a worker and employer designed to prevent the worker from making a protected disclosure is void. This includes agreements, such as Compromise Agreements, not to commence or continue proceedings for breach of contract or proceedings under the Public Interest Disclosure Act 1998

43K. – (1) For the purposes of this Part "worker" includes an individual who is not a worker as defined by section 230(3) but who-

(a) works or worked for a person in circumstances in which-
  (i) he is or was introduced or supplied to do that work by a third person, and
  (ii) the terms on which he is or was engaged to do the work are or were in practice substantially determined not by him but by the person for whom he works or worked, by the third person or by both of them,

(b) contracts or contracted with a person, for the purposes of that person's business, for the execution of work to be done in a place not under the control or management of that person and would fall within section 230(3)(b) if for "personally" in that provision there were substituted "(whether personally or otherwise)",

(c) works or worked as a person providing general medical services, general dental services, general ophthalmic services or pharmaceutical services in accordance with arrangements made-
  (i) by a Health Authority under section 29, 35, 38 or 41 of the National Health Service Act 1977, or
  (ii) by a Health Board under section 19, 25, 26 or 27 of the National Health Service (Scotland) Act 1978, or

(d) is or was provided with work experience provided pursuant to a training course or programme or with training for employment (or with both) otherwise than-
  (i) under a contract of employment, or
  (ii) by an educational establishment on a course run by that establishment;

and any reference to a worker's contract, to employment or to a worker being "employed" shall be construed accordingly.

(2) For the purposes of this Part "employer" includes-

(a) in relation to a worker falling within paragraph (a) of subsection (1), the person who substantially determines or determined the terms on which he is or was engaged,

(b) in relation to a worker falling within paragraph (c) of that subsection, the authority or board referred to in that paragraph, and

(c) in relation to a worker falling within paragraph (d) of that subsection, the person providing the work experience or training.

(3) In this section "educational establishment" includes any university, college, school or other educational establishment.

The definition of "worker" includes "employees" and "workers" as defined by the Employment Rights Act 1996 and is wide. It includes not only "employees" and "workers" under the Employment Rights Act 1996 but also a worker who would otherwise be outside the scope of the Employment Rights Act 1996 but meets qualifying conditions set out in s.43K - primarily this work is controlled by third party contractors. Workers also include dentists and doctors under statutory schemes and individuals working under certain training contracts

43L. – (1) In this Part-

"qualifying disclosure" has the meaning given by section 43B;

"the relevant failure", in relation to a qualifying disclosure, has the meaning given by section 43B(5).

(2) In determining for the purposes of this Part whether a person makes a disclosure for purposes of personal gain, there shall be disregarded any reward payable by or under any enactment.

(3) Any reference in this Part to the disclosure of information shall have effect, in relation to any case where the person receiving the information is already aware of it, as a reference to bringing the information to his attention."

2. After section 47A of the 1996 Act there is inserted-

S.2 - S.47B is inserted into the Employment Rights Act 1996 providing a right not to suffer detriment as a consequence of making a protected disclosure. The concept of what amounts to a "detriment" is well established by case law, particularly in the field of Equal Opportunities legislation

"47B. – (1) A worker has the right not to be subjected to any detriment by any act, or any deliberate failure to act, by his employer done on the ground that the worker has made a protected disclosure.

(2) Except where the worker is an employee who is dismissed in circumstances in which, by virtue of section 197, Part X does not apply to the dismissal, this section does not apply where-

(a) the worker is an employee, and
(b) the detriment in question amounts to dismissal (within the meaning of that Part).

(3) For the purposes of this section, and of sections 48 and 49 so far as relating to this section, "worker", "worker's contract", "employment" and "employer" have the extended meaning given by section 43K."

3. In section 48 of the 1996 Act (complaints to employment tribunals), after subsection (1) there is inserted-

> *S.3 - Complaints that rights given by the Public Interest Disclosure Act 1998 have been violated are made to the Employment Tribunal*

"(1A) A worker may present a complaint to an employment tribunal that he has been subjected to a detriment in contravention of section 47B."

4. – (1) Section 49 of the 1996 Act (remedies) is amended as follows.

(2) At the beginning of subsection (2) there is inserted "Subject to subsection (6)".

> *S.4 – This section provides for the upper limits on compensation. The remedies provided under Part V of the Employment Rights Act 1996 (protection from suffering detriment in employment) are amended to provide for complaints under the Public Interest Disclosure Act 1998 with related limits on the amount of compensation. However the Public Interest Disclosure (Compensation) Order 1999 SI.1999/1548 which came into force on 2 July 1999 removes the upper limit on compensation following acceptance that the proposed upper limit of £50,000 would act as a disincentive to highly paid individuals making protected disclosures.*

(3) After subsection (5) there is inserted-

" (6) Where-

(a) the complaint is made under section 48(1A),

    (b) the detriment to which the worker is subjected is the termination of his worker's contract, and

    (c) that contract is not a contract of employment,

any compensation must not exceed the compensation that would be payable under Chapter II of Part X if the worker had been an employee and had been dismissed for the reason specified in section 103A."

5. After section 103 of the 1996 Act there is inserted-

> *S.5 - The dismissal of an employee for making a protected disclosure is automatically an unfair dismissal. Accordingly the Tribunal is not required to consider whether the employer's actions were reasonable. There is no qualifying period of one year's service nor an upper age limit. Where the worker is not an employee a complaint is made to the Tribunal under s.3*

"Protected disclosure.

103A. An employee who is dismissed shall be regarded for the purposes of this Part as unfairly dismissed if the reason (or, if more than one, the principal reason) for the dismissal is that the employee made a protected disclosure."

6. After subsection (6) of section 105 of the 1996 Act (redundancy) there is inserted-

> *S.6 - The selection of an employee for dismissal by reason of redundancy is automatically an unfair dismissal where the reason for the selection was that the employee had made a protected disclosure*

"(6A) This subsection applies if the reason (or, if more than one, the principal reason) for which the employee was selected for dismissal was that specified in section 103A."

7. – (1) In subsection (3) of section 108 of the 1996 Act (cases where qualifying period of employment not required), after paragraph (f) there is inserted-

> *S.7 - The protection against unfair dismissal is s.5 and s.6 are not dependent upon one year's qualifying service and is not lost if an employee remains in employment beyond the upper age limit*

"(ff) section 103A applies,"

(2) In subsection (2) of section 109 of the 1996 Act (disapplication of upper age limit), after paragraph (f) there is inserted-

"(ff) section 103A applies,".

8. – (1) In section 112(4) of the 1996 Act (compensation for unfair dismissal) after "sections 118 to 127A" there is inserted "or in accordance with regulations under section 127B".

> ***S.8(1)*** *- The requirement that an Employment Tribunal shall make an award of compensation for unfair dismissal where reinstatement or re-engagement are not ordered is extended to cover the provisions of the Public Interest Disclosure Act 1998*

(2) In section 117 of that Act (enforcement of order for reinstatement or re-engagement)-

    (a) in subsection (2) after "section 124" there is inserted "and to regulations under section 127B", and

    (b) in subsection (3) after "and (2)" there is inserted "and to regulations under section 127B".

> ***S.8(2)*** *- The discretionary remedies for unfair dismissal of reinstatement and re-engagement are extended to cover an unfair dismissal*

(3) In section 118 of that Act (general provisions as to unfair dismissal), at the beginning of subsection (1) there is inserted "Subject to regulations under section 127B,".

> ***S.8(3)*** *- The compensation machinery of basic awards, compensatory awards and special awards are extended to dismissals as a result of a protected disclosure*

(4) After section 127A of the 1996 Act there is inserted-

"127B. – (1) This section applies where the reason (or, if more than one, the principal reason)-

    (a) in a redundancy case, for selecting the employee for dismissal, or

(b) otherwise, for the dismissal,

is that specified in section 103A.

(2) The Secretary of State may by regulations provide that where this section applies any award of compensation for unfair dismissal under section 112(4) or 117(1) or 117(3) shall, instead of being calculated in accordance with the provisions of sections 117 to 127A, consist of one or more awards calculated in such manner as may be prescribed by the regulations.

(3) Regulations under this section may, in particular, apply any of the provisions of sections 117 to 127A with such modifications as may be specified in the regulations."

S.8(4) - The Secretary of State may introduce Regulations providing for a difference basis of calculation of the compensation award for dismissal as a result of a protected disclosure. The Public Interest Disclosure (Compensation) Order 1999 came into force on 2 July 1999

9. In sections 128(1)(b) and 129(1) of the 1996 Act (which relate to interim relief) for "or 103" there is substituted ", 103 or 103A".

S.9 - Where a worker presents a complaint to an Employment Tribunal alleging dismissal as a result of a protected disclosure, an application can be made for interim relief - either interim reinstatement, re-engagement or continuation of the employee's contract of employment - pending the full merits hearing and final determination of the complaint. The Employment Tribunal may make such orders if it appears to the Tribunal at the interim relief hearing that it is likely that the outcome of the full merits hearing that the Applicant was dismissed as a result of a protected disclosure

10. In section 191 of the 1996 Act (Crown employment), in subsection (2) after paragraph (a) there is inserted-

S.10 - Crown employment is brought within the scope of the Act subject to certain exceptions

"(aa) Part IVA,".

11. – (1) Section 193 of the 1996 Act (national security) is amended as follows.

S.11 - Certain categories of Crown employment are excluded from the scope of the Act on the grounds of national security including employment in the Security Service, the Secret Intelligence Service or the Government Communications Headquarters

(2) In subsection (2) after paragraph (b) there is inserted-

"(bb) Part IVA,

(bc) in Part V, section 47B,".

(3) After subsection (3) of that section there is inserted-

"(4) Part IVA and sections 47B and 103A do not have effect in relation to employment for the purposes of the Security Service, the Secret Intelligence Service or the Government Communications Headquarters."

12. – (1) Section 196 of the 1996 Act (employment outside Great Britain) is amended as follows.

S.12 - The Act is disapplied where the worker ordinarily works outside Great Britain

(2) After subsection (3) there is inserted-

"(3A) Part IVA and section 47B do not apply to employment where under the worker's contract he ordinarily works outside Great Britain."

(3) In subsection (5), after "subsections (2)" there is inserted ", (3A)".

13. In section 200 of the 1996 Act (police officers), in subsection (1) (which lists provisions of the Act which do not apply to employment under a contract of employment in police service, or to persons engaged in such employment)-

S.13 - The application of the Act in respect of Police Officers is restricted

(a) after "Part III" there is inserted ", Part IVA", and
(b) after "47" there is inserted ", 47B".

14. In section 205 of the 1996 Act (remedy for infringement of certain rights) after subsection (1) there is inserted-

> **S.14** - *A complaint of infringement of rights under the Act can only be brought before an Employment Tribunal*

"(1A) In relation to the right conferred by section 47B, the reference in subsection (1) to an employee has effect as a reference to a worker."

15. – (1) At the end of section 230 of the 1996 Act (employees, workers etc) there is inserted-

> **S.15** - *This section adds the definitions under this Act e.g. "Worker" and "Protected Disclosure" to the comprehensive list of definitions set out in s.230 of the Employment Rights Act 1996*

"(6) This section has effect subject to sections 43K and 47B(3); and for the purposes of Part XIII so far as relating to Part IVA or section 47B, "worker", "worker's contract" and, in relation to a worker, "employer", "employment" and "employed" have the extended meaning given by section 43K."

(2) In section 235 of the 1996 Act (other definitions) after the definition of "position" there is inserted-

" "protected disclosure" has the meaning given by section 43A,".

16. – (1) In section 237 of the Trade Union and Labour Relations (Consolidation) Act 1992 (dismissal of those taking part in unofficial industrial action), in subsection (1A) (which provides that the exclusion of the right to complain of unfair dismissal does not apply in certain cases)-

> **S.16** - *Section 237 of the Trade Union & Labour Relations (Consolidation) Act 1992 provides that those who are dismissed for taking part in unofficial industrial action cannot make a complaint of unfair dismissal to an Employment Tribunal. That provision is disapplied in certain cases and the exception in respect of "employee representative" cases is extended to include protected disclosure cases*

(a) for "or 103" there is substituted ", 103 or 103A", and

(b) for "and employee representative cases)" there is substituted "employee representative and protected disclosure cases)".

17. An Order in Council under paragraph 1(1)(b) of Schedule 1 to the Northern Ireland Act 1974 (legislation for Northern Ireland in the interim period) which states that it is made only for purposes corresponding to those of this Act-

> **S.17** - *Arrangements for a corresponding provision for Northern Ireland*

(a) shall not be subject to paragraph 1(4) and (5) of that Schedule (affirmative resolution of both Houses of Parliament), but
(b) shall be subject to annulment in pursuance of a resolution of either House of Parliament.

18. – (1) This Act may be cited as the Public Interest Disclosure Act 1998.

> **S.18** - *Provides the short title for this Act as the Public Interest Disclosure Act 1998 and for the commencement of dates to be appointed by the Secretary of State. With effect from 2 July 1998 the Secretary of State is empowered to make "prescribed persons" and "compensation" orders and corresponding provisions under s.17 for Northern Ireland. This Act does not extend to Northern Ireland other than the enabling provisions in s.17 for corresponding provisions for Northern Ireland*

(2) In this Act "the 1996 Act" means the Employment Rights Act 1996.

(3) Subject to subsection (4), this Act shall come into force on such day or days as the Secretary of State may by order made by statutory instrument appoint, and different days may be appointed for different purposes.

(4) The following provisions shall come into force on the passing of this Act-

(a) section 1 so far as relating to the power to make an order under section 43F of the 1996 Act,
(b) section 8 so far as relating to the power to make regulations under section 127B of the 1996 Act,
(c) section 17, and
(d) this section.

(5) This Act, except section 17, does not extend to Northern Ireland.

Index

Index by George Curzon,
Indexing Specialists